SUSTAINABLE DESIGN S

David E. Miller, *Series Editor*

MW01201859

ARCHITECTS OF THE PACIFIC NORTHWEST HAVE BEEN CELEBRATED FOR A long-standing respect for the environment and a holistic view of their place in it. This series spotlights innovative design achievements by contemporary Northwest architects, and supporting consultants, whose work reinforces core principles and ethics of sustainable design. Reflecting cross-disciplinary inspirations ranging from environmental sciences to sociology and systems biology, the pioneering buildings and technologies profiled in this series share common aesthetic and social goals. Promoting maximum energy efficiency through extensive use of recycled materials and minimal dependence on mechanical systems for heat, ventilation, and waste management, these works demonstrate a profound and enduring love of the natural world and its ecological systems.

Studio at Large:
Architecture in Service of Global Communities
by Sergio Palleroni, with Christina Eichbaum Merkelbach

Toward a New Regionalism:
Environmental Architecture in the Pacific Northwest
by David E. Miller

Daylighting Design in the Pacific Northwest
by Christopher M. Meek and Kevin G. Van Den Wymelenberg

UNIVERSITY OF WASHINGTON PRESS *Seattle and London*

DAYLIGHTING DESIGN IN THE PACIFIC NORTHWEST

CHRISTOPHER M. MEEK

KEVIN G. VAN DEN WYMELENBERG

FOREWORD BY JOEL E. LOVELAND

Daylighting Design in the Pacific Northwest is published with the assistance of a grant from the University of Washington Architecture Publications Fund. The Northwest Energy Efficiency Alliance and the College of Built Environments, Dean's Office, University of Washington, provided additional support.

© 2012 by the University of Washington Press
Printed and bound in China
Design by Thomas Eykemans
Composed in Univers, typeface designed by Adrian Frutiger
16 15 14 13 12   5 4 3 2 1

University of Washington Press
PO Box 50096, Seattle, WA 98145, USA
www.washington.edu/uwpress

Library of Congress Cataloging-in-Publication Data
Meek, Christopher (Christopher Martin), 1971–
Daylighting design in the Pacific Northwest /
Christopher M. Meek and Kevin G. Van Den Wymelenberg ;
foreword by Joel Loveland. — 1st [edition].
    pages cm — (Sustainable design solutions from the Pacific Northwest)
Includes index.
ISBN 978-0-295-99206-8 (pbk : alk. paper)
1. Daylighting—Northwest, Pacific—Case studies.
2. Sustainable architecture—Northwest, Pacific—Case studies.
I. Van Den Wymelenberg, Kevin G.
II. Title.
NA2794.M44 2012   720′.47—dc23   2012009926

The paper used in this publication meets the minimum requirements of American National Standard for Information Sciences—Permanence of Paper for Printed Library Materials, ANSI Z39.48-1984.∞

Contents

Foreword

TO LIVE IN THE PACIFIC NORTHWEST IS TO KNOW SUMMER'S LONG LOW LIGHT and winter's long dark nights. To live with this light is to understand one's place in the landscape, and to design with it is to sense how the rhythm of light defines the rhythms of our lives.

The unique daylight of Cascadia is luscious, soft, and translucent. The cool breath of the Pacific nudges its moisture inland to provide a blanket of insulating and light-diffusing clouds, which are trapped by the mountainous Cascade rim. This atmosphere creates a lush landscape and a place of abundant resources.

The light of day and a view of the sky have always been at a premium in this dim and deeply wooded natural landscape. Amidst trees so large that nineteenth-century immigrants balked at the task of cutting them, both Native peoples and settlers made their homes at the edges of forests in search of light and prospect.

Modern architecture, too, celebrates daylight—and darkness. Generations of modern architects and landscape architects, along with their clients, have evolved a design vocabulary of open choreography anchored in the spirituality of the northern coastal culture of long spring-summer days and protracted autumn-winter nights. In recent years, Scandinavian immigrant traditions have combined with the dramatic, open, and transparent Pacific Northwest architecture of the mid-twentieth century to form a highly refined hybrid style.

Today, the Pacific Northwest is defined by a profound concern for the ecological footprint we are leaving on our landscape, and the region has developed some of the nation's most forward-looking codes of ecological design practice. Architects in the Pacific Northwest have learned to adapt the regional design tradition to increase energy efficiency while maintaining the rich illumination of daylight. The new designs make innovative use of carefully placed small apertures of light from the side and, most luscious of all, the skylight.

This wonderful book documents the practice of daylighting in the world-class architecture of a unique group of Pacific Northwest Coast–based architects. It shows how this practice has evolved to celebrate the ecology of daylight and the building traditions it has inspired.

Joel E. Loveland
Director, Integrated Design Lab
Department of Architecture
University of Washington

Preface

WE ARE FORTUNATE TO HAVE HAD THE OPPORTUNITY TO LEAD A UNIQUE type of academic position, one based on the fusion of academic research, professional practice, and teaching with some of the best design practitioners and students in the Pacific Northwest. In the university context, most of our work is characterized as applied research and project-based educational outreach. In the eyes of the design professionals, our work is characterized as building-science research and technical design assistance. This type of engagement has built a bridge between the design professions and the academy and helped develop a body of knowledge in building science and a range of built works of architecture that we feel are important to document.

By emphasizing the functional, dynamic, and dramatic qualities that the innovative use of daylight can bring to our experience of the built environment, this book aims to motivate architects, engineers, and lighting designers to become reacquainted with the art of designing with daylight as the primary source of illumination.

Acknowledgments

WE WOULD LIKE TO THANK THE DESIGN TEAMS WHO ALLOWED US TO BE PART of their process. We also acknowledge the Betterbricks program of the Northwest Energy Efficiency Alliance for the generous support that enabled our contribution to these projects and for its commitment to this book, as well as the Dean's Office at the University of Washington College of Built Environments, which provided publication support.

Very special thanks go to Professor Joel Loveland for his leadership of the Pacific Northwest Integrated Design Lab Network, his mentorship over the past decade, and his tireless dedication to the promotion of daylighting in buildings. Thanks to all the lab staff who supported design and analysis of projects included in this book, especially Martin Brennan, Maximillian Foley, Gunnar Gladics, Sarah Marshall, Macy Miller, Susan Olmstead, Tristan Van Slyke, and Carl Von Rueden. We would also like to thank David Miller, Beth Fuget, and John Jennings for their support of this book, as well as Jeffrey Ochsner, Lisa Heschong, Gwynneth Harris, Dwaine Carver, and Laura Iwasaki for their guidance on the manuscript. We are grateful to Lorri Hagman and Thomas Eykemans at the University of Washington Press for production support and design. Special thanks to GSBS Architects, HKP Architects, KPG Architects and Engineers, Mahlum, the Miller Hull Partnership, McKibben + Cooper Architects, Mithun, Olson Kundig Architects, Trout Architects, Weber + Thompson, and Weinstein AIU.

Plan and section drawings, adapted from drawings provided by the designers, are by Kalan Beck, Nick Hubof, and Sean Kelley.

Daylighting Design in the Pacific Northwest

Introduction

BUILDING DESIGN IS INHERENTLY THE DESIGN OF LIGHTING. ARCHITECTURAL decisions, including building orientation, aperture placement and size, interior geometry, and surface characteristics combine with the ever-changing light of the sky to form distinct and dynamic luminous conditions. A patch of sunlight marks the passage of time, and diffuse daylight swells as the vapor of an overhead cloud dissipates. These phenomena connect us to the authentic nature of place and to the rhythm of light and dark that shapes our being in the world. Daylight breathes light and life into our buildings. Daylight and sunlight are perhaps the last refuge of true wildness in our modern cities. As Thoreau put it, "In wildness is the preservation of the world."[1]

The projects featured in this book represent what we think are the best daylighting efforts in the current wave of sustainable design practice in the Pacific Northwest. They were selected because each presents us with new knowledge about synthesizing the light of place with the specific needs of human activity. This book is intended to bridge the "monograph" culture of the design world and the density of traditional building-science texts in a format that both inspires and instructs.

Most projects included in this book are public buildings, since commercial and institutional buildings offer the best opportunities for designers who want to use daylight as a functional light source, something that has been rare since the 1940s; at the same time, they also present the greatest challenge. Daylighting is a regionally specific activity. Its design requires the interplay of form, space, and materiality derived from the influence of site, climate, regional culture, and the distinct requirements of specific visual tasks. Nevertheless, the conceptual ideas employed in the projects illustrated herein are broadly applicable to a wide range of building designs that seek to create high-quality interior environments with daylight.

As authors, the primary challenge we face in presenting this work is in the visual representation of dynamic phenomena. The current convention in architectural photography is to capture scenes at twilight, the "magic hour," with all electric lighting on, when the visual contrast between indoor and outdoor light levels is low and drama is high. This can create compelling imagery but runs contrary to our intentions. Our goal is to show interior spaces under the patterns of daylight present during more typical times in the use of the building. We also used daylight as the primary, and usually the only, source of light in our exposures. In our photographs, the ambient electric lighting is off so that the reader might more clearly see the distribution of daylight created by the architecture itself. In order to achieve a successful and authentic representation of the daylight distribution within these interiors, we used the relatively new technique of high dynamic range (HDR) photography. We feel that HDR imaging, with its capability to represent luminous contrast, enables a depiction of interior space that is close to the way the human eye perceives it. Therefore, we believe it is the most appropriate method for illustrating the nature of daylight delivered by the architecture itself and for reflecting the intention of the designs: to create places where the luminous requirements of human activity are met primarily with daylight.

Many readers will see the images and say, "This is just one moment in time. How does the space perform in the late afternoon in December?" We recognize this challenge and agree with its premise. In this book, we are chasing light with words and photographs. The truth is in the firsthand experience of the architecture through time. Our hope is that this work encourages readers to reassess the functional potential of daylight in buildings and embrace the dynamic qualities that make daylit spaces so compelling. Our intention is to inspire designers and building users alike to raise the level of their expectations about what a daylit space is and to provide instruction on how to improve daylight design in buildings through an examination of successful examples.

LIGHT OF PLACE IN THE PACIFIC NORTHWEST

The sky is mostly gray. From October until June, the Pacific Northwest is cast in an even, milky, consistent light, sometimes called "oyster light," which magnifies the deep green of the natural landscape. It is not a transient condition; it is the dominant one.

—David E. Miller, *Toward a New Regionalism*[2]

The Pacific Northwest is legendary for its overcast skies, but closer inspection reveals a multivariate region with a wide range of sky cover and distinct seasonal patterns of clouds and sun. Understanding these phenomena and the contexts they create is crucial to the design of daylight-responsive architecture in this region and elsewhere. The unique character of the Northwest sky results from the juxtaposition of glacial and volcanic mountain formations and the North Pacific Ocean weather systems that dominate the area. The combination of these landscape elements and meteorological forces creates a distinctly regional distribution and quality of daylight. Cliff Mass, professor of atmospheric sciences at the University of Washington, offers the following description in his book *The Weather of the Pacific Northwest*: "Startling weather contrasts over small distances are some of the most singular aspects of Northwest weather. The high terrain of the region often separates radically different climate and weather regimes, with transitions occurring over a matter of miles." He adds that

if one could use a single phrase to describe Pacific Northwest weather, "wet and mild" would be a start, but not a particularly exact one. Although the region west of the Cascade crest is considered "wet" by many, it enjoys some of the driest summers in the nation and receives less annual precipitation than much of the eastern United States. East of the Cascades, where arid conditions dominate, "wet" is certainly not an apt description, and east-side temperature extremes, ranging from −48 to 119°F, makes "mild" a misnomer at times. Northwest weather and climate are dominated by two main elements: (1) the vast Pacific Ocean to the west and (2) the region's mountain ranges that block and deflect low-level air.[3]

In the Pacific Northwest, as the jet stream pushes air from the west inland to the east, clouds form on the western slopes of major mountains, including the Cascade Range, and clearing occurs to the east. Long-term weather data indicate that Seattle and Portland, both west of the Cascades, are overcast nearly 230 days per year, but the inland cities of Spokane, Washington, and Boise, Idaho, are overcast only 191 and 155 days per year on average respectively. Overlaid on the contrasting character of areas west and east of the Cascades is a distinct seasonal shift between cloudy winter months to a dominantly clear sky period between July and October—this pattern is most apparent west of the Cascades. The annual periodicity of overcast and sun, caused by shifts in the jet stream over the Pacific Ocean, combines with mild year-round ocean temperatures to amplify precipitation in winter and inhibit it during the summer months.[4]

The physical and visual experiences of climate in the inland Pacific Northwest are different from those in the maritime coastal areas. Consequently, each subregion's daylight has its own characteristics. A common experience east of the Cascades is the golden glow of low-angle late summer sun that reaches across burned sagebrush-cloaked foothills and paints the ridges light umber and the valleys dark umber during the early morning and late afternoon and a vibrant gold at midday. In contrast, the forested coastal regions of the maritime Northwest are defined largely by the inverted topography of cloud cover. Here, mild temperatures predominate, and steely silver-gray

Cloudscape. Photo: Mary Randlett, *Cloud Form #1*, September 1998. Courtesy Special Collections, University of Washington

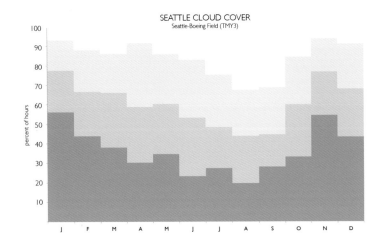

SEATTLE CLOUD COVER
Seattle–Boeing Field (TMY3)

percent of hours

□ clear
  scattered clouds
  broken clouds
■ overcast

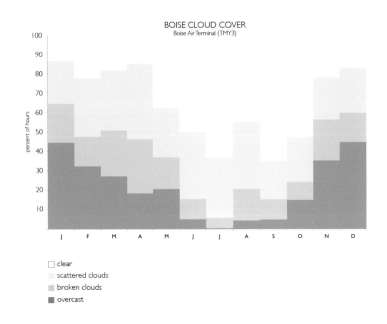

BOISE CLOUD COVER
Boise Air Terminal (TMY3)

percent of hours

□ clear
  scattered clouds
  broken clouds
■ overcast

Monthly and annual sky cover range in Seattle from data for a typical meteorological year (TMY). Source: U.S. Department of Energy, http://apps1.eere.energy.gov/buildings/energyplus/cfm/weather_data.cfm (retrieved 9 Sept. 2011). Likely percentage of cloud cover in Seattle from January through December. These data show typical Pacific Northwest patterns of overcast from October through June with substantially more likelihood of clear skies in July, August, and September.

Monthly and annual sky cover range in Boise from data for a typical meteorological year (TMY). Source: U.S. Department of Energy, http://apps1.eere.energy.gov/buildings/energyplus/cfm/weather_data.cfm (retrieved 9 Sept. 2011).

and muted violet provide an ever-changing ceiling of "oyster light." In this microclimate, a winter morning sky begins dark blue, sometimes with a thin, banded warm reveal at the horizon where the milky cloud layer peels back from the earth's edge to allow a brief peek of the morning sun. This temporary warm reveal lies beyond the mountains on the distant horizon and quickly fades to gray as the sun passes behind the lid formed by the heavy blue-gray cloud layer. Following these general distinctions, the light of place in the Northwest must be considered in at least two major categories as established by sky conditions on each side of the Cascade Range.

Despite these important and local climate differences, common themes bind this regional context in terms of daylighting design considerations. One is the northern latitude of the Pacific Northwest, which provides commonality in terms of solar angles and annual daylight hours. Another is the predominance of the overcast sky. Even the sunnier cities of the inland Northwest pass a substantial period of the year under overcast skies.

Finally, the exceptional topography throughout much of the region plays a role in the architectural response to the connection with both earth and sky. Building on hillsides creates an intimate eye-level connection with the sky that is not experienced in comparatively flat landscapes. In major cities such as Seattle, Portland, and parts of Boise and Spokane, building with the topography results in distant views that encompass a large portion of the sky.

Overarching climate and landscape conditions such as these can be described and understood through empirical data, yet an informed understanding of the specific *visual* (and *thermal*) *phenomena* created by the atmosphere and landscape is critical for designing with daylight. Regional weather patterns broadly shape designers' understanding of climate, but important microclimate phenomena such as site-specific solar access, overshadowing from adjacent structures and landforms, and the likelihood of cloud cover relative to typical outdoor air temperatures must also

Pacific Northwest inland landscape. Photo: K. Van Den Wymelenberg.

Maritime cloud cover over the San Juan Islands, Washington. Photo: C. Meek.

Sunbreak over Seattle. Photo: C. Meek.

Polar sun angles for latitude 47° north.

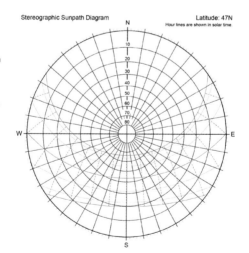

Stereographic Sunpath Diagram

Latitude: 47N
Hour lines are shown in solar time.

be considered in grasping the daylighting context of a building. Successful daylighting design synthesizes all of these phenomena with the needs of the building's occupants.

Despite the influential climate design factors described above, concepts of light in early Pacific Northwest urban buildings were largely European models of construction transplanted via American cities in the East and Midwest. These traditions of building design and construction include prescribed relationships between windows, floor plate depth, and building organization. Initially expressed as heavy-timber and masonry buildings, early construction in the Northwest later gave way to concrete, steel, and terra-cotta. Although these historic buildings continue to be in high demand and have served a wide variety of functions over time, their success lies more in universally sound design principles than in a specific response to the Northwest landscape or climate. In this regard, building culture and its relationship to daylight did not develop a distinct regional character until the emergence of Northwest Modernism and the Northwest School in the postwar era, led by University of Washington professor Lionel Pries and architects Paul Thiry, Paul Hayden Kirk, and Pietro Belluschi. Influenced by the indoor-outdoor duality of the Japanese vernacular and the direct material expression of European Modernism, a distinctly Northwest regional modernism began to take shape. With its immediate relationship to the landscape and formal dialogue with the sun and sky, this strain of Modernism has set the course for much of the region's significant works of architecture.

Until recently, the same global and national influences that brought Modernism to the Pacific Northwest also brought a near-total reliance on electric light sources for interior illumination. In order to more completely understand the context in which daylight is reemerging as a formative influence on building design, we offer a discussion of the cultural and technological influences that underpin the role of daylight in buildings in the Northwest.

RE-PLACING DAYLIGHT IN THE ARCHITECTURE OF BUILDINGS: A PROBLEM STATEMENT

Much of the modern world has been assembled as if people were machines without deeper needs for order, pattern, and roots. Modern designers filled the world with buildings and developments divorced from their context, existing as if in some alien realm disconnected from ecology, history, culture, people, and place.[5]

—David Orr, Oberlin College

The past decade has seen a reawakening to the central role that daylight can play in our interior environments and the design of our buildings. As concepts of eco-consciousness and localism have wound their way into the contemporary zeitgeist, design professionals have rediscovered daylight as a primary site resource for energy efficiency, function, and beauty in their work. Research by Lisa Heschong and others suggests that the inclusion of daylight and views in our built environment leads to better outcomes in education, healing, and work environments.[6] Concurrently, new developments in the emerging science of photobiology and research into the relationship between daylight and human productivity are beginning to reveal the unintended consequences of a world unregulated by the light of day.[7] In a culture in which the the quantification of lightness and space is elusive, these developments offer a new path toward a broader and more inclusive understanding of the dynamic luminous quality that daylight offers in buildings.

Many of the assumptions that currently form the starting point for typical commercial and institutional buildings preclude the widespread use of daylight as a functional light source. Very deep office floor plates that place occupants far from windows are designed to maximize leasable space. Persistent ingrained hierarchies dictate providing highly glazed offices for a few senior managers while leaving the majority of occupants in windowless "cubicle farms."

Hospitals are notorious for confining nursing and other caregiver staff to workstations located deep in the center of buildings, where they spend entire shifts with no access to windows. Many school districts have adopted a model for classrooms that maximizes section depth in order to reduce corridor costs and has had the effect of making it nearly impossible to provide sufficient daylight without skylights, which are often expressly prohibited. Given that daylight and views are universally identified by building inhabitants as a positive design element, why do so many of the fundamental assumptions that shape our building types today discourage the use of daylight as a primary source of illumination?

Architecture's daylight deprivation happened relatively recently. As little as 150 years ago, daylight and burning oil were the sole sources of illumination in our interior environments. Humans awoke and slept by the cycles of daylight, with minimal intervention from man-made light sources. Regional climate phenomena, including wind flows, air temperature, precipitation, and patterns of daylight, drove building design. Spaces of human habitation implicitly resonated with their environmental context. Daylight was the primary source of illumination, and human reliance on the light of day dramatically affected our experience of the world.

"ARTIFICIAL" LIGHT VS. DAYLIGHT

A culture in which artificial light is available will have a means of extending the day and as a consequence will experience the world differently than a culture without artificial light.

—Karin Knorr Cetina[8]

Technological advances in heating, cooling, ventilating, and lighting during the first half of the twentieth century ushered in an era of unheard-of comfort and control. These developments offered architects a new formal freedom, allowing designers to forgo centuries-old geometric relationships

Windowless industrial facility. Photo: Eric Strandberg, Lighting Design Lab.

Interior partitions block all daylight and views from this workstation.
Photo: Joel Loveland.

that served to provide light and air to building occupants. The reshaping of architecture in response to technological advances and cheap sources of energy is most prominently documented in Reyner Banham's 1969 book *The Architecture of the Well-Tempered Environment*. The decoupling from climate-responsive and regionalist architecture Banham describes might have resulted in buildings that afforded a greater dialogue with the immediate physical context, yet such was rarely the case. More often, buildings became self-contained environments that suppressed human sensory experience and depreciated the visceral (if sometimes harsh and uncomfortable) intimacy with the outdoor world that humanity once experienced. Rather than becoming mired in the complexity of the human visual system, many building designers abandoned the notion that daylight could form the primary basis for space illumination, rendering its use unnecessary and, from some perspectives, even undesirable.

Daylight is highly variable, and it is inextricably intertwined with darkness. These characteristics do not meet the simplified and easily quantifiable standards of constant horizontal foot-candles that typically govern the science of illuminating engineering. Furthermore, current human expectations of thermal and visual comfort developed in tandem with the characteristics of mechanized systems of illumination. Cheap, abundant energy has driven the rapid, widespread adoption and deployment of climate control technology, and the notion of a steady state interior environment has become commonplace. As building occupants have become accustomed to the constancy and stability of mechanical and electrical climate controls, human conceptions and expectations of comfort in buildings have become far more constricted. A culture seduced by mechanization and confident that technology will always deliver meaningful progress has readily accepted this dramatic shift to an unvarying, existential comfort flat-line. In this context, daylight as a source of functional illumination has become marginalized, and the indoor environment subsequently has become more commodified, interchangeable, and less regionally specific.

Portlandia Building, Portland, Oregon.
Photo: Steve Morgan.

Venetian Hotel Casino shopping mall,
Las Vegas. Photo: C. Meek.

A twenty-four-hour metropolis has evolved, to the point that there is very little noticeable differentiation between day and night in many interior spaces. We have the ability to light everything, all the time, and we often do. Anyone who has flown above a major metropolis at night has seen the acres of empty parking lots, vacant ball fields, and shuttered strip malls that are nevertheless illuminated against the unacceptable encroachment of darkness. In this sense, much of our luminous experience of the world has been flattened into a sort of *netherworld*, a place of permanent twilight.

Technological innovation and changing cultural expectations about the indoor environment do not by themselves explain the predicament of disconnected interior environments. As energy codes emerged in the 1970s as a result of the 1973 oil embargo, windows came to be viewed as a liability primarily due to heat gain and heat loss. Since windows were no longer designed to produce tangible results for space illumination, many structures were simply built with smaller windows. As a result, early energy-efficiency efforts too often resulted in buildings that were even less comfortable than their predecessors. Reductions in comfort were often compounded with reduced requirements for fresh air in the name of efficiency. Small, "energy-efficient" punched openings provided modest view allowances, which in turn caused excessive glare with relatively dark surrounding surfaces. This kind of design sometimes produces interiors in which window blinds are deployed during all daylight hours, yielding the worst of all scenarios: spaces with no views, no daylight, and a thermal penalty for the use of glass rather than opaque wall. The logical conclusion to this mode of energy efficiency is to build windowless superinsulated boxes with "ultra-efficient" mechanized climate control systems. Despite the prevailing trend toward climate-rejecting buildings in the latter part of the twentieth century, several iconic daylit buildings were built in the Pacific Northwest during that time. Most notable is Alvar Aalto's library at the Mount Angel Abbey in Oregon, which reasserts the possibilities of interior space, light, and movement. The work of Cana-

dian architect Arthur Erickson has been similarly influential, including his 1976 Museum of Anthropology at the University of British Columbia and the British Columbia Provincial Law Courts in downtown Vancouver, designed in 1973.

In recent decades, we have seen a change in attitude away from the reductive approach to energy efficiency that tended to suppress daylight in our habitable spaces. This shift is due in large part to user dissatisfaction and poor indoor environmental quality resulting from building designs that treat windows solely as an energy liability. Climate and regional context are being broadly recast as resources to be employed and engaged in the design process rather than simply fortified against. Daylight is at the forefront of this shift because it provides an immediately tangible connection to the outdoors and its use does not have to constitute a zero-sum trade-off. When effectively integrated with building design, daylight provides higher-quality indoor environments *and* greater energy efficiency.

The early work of John and Patricia Patkau, of Patkau Architects, and David Miller and Robert Hull, of the Miller Hull Partnership, has taken the architectural possibility of daylight demonstrated through Pacific Northwest iconic forms from the likes of Aalto and Erickson and embedded it in more common building types. Buildings such as the Patkaus' Newton Library, from 1992, in Surrey, and Strawberry Vale Elementary School, from 1995, in Victoria, British Columbia, and Miller Hull's Water Pollution Control Laboratory, from 1997, in Portland, Oregon, are a few examples of how the skillful use of daylight can transform common building types into extraordinary architectural experiences.

The design teams and projects showcased in the following chapters build on these successes, continue to push back against the tide of increased standardization within our interior environments, and seek to recover the local light of day. They illustrate the mechanisms by which buildings influence cultural connections to nature and how design, and

Opposite:

Alvar Aalto's Mount Angel Abbey Library, Saint Benedict, Oregon, completed 1970. Photo: Nick Hubof/University of Idaho Integrated Design Lab.

Interior of the British Columbia Provincial Law Courts, Vancouver, designed by Arthur Erickson, 1973. Photo: Joel Loveland.

Exterior view of the main gallery at the Museum of Anthropology at the University of British Columbia, Vancouver, by Arthur Erickson, completed in 1976. Photo: Buchanan-Hermit.

Interior view of skylight and *The Raven and the First Men*, by Bill Reid, at the Museum of Anthropology. Photo: Joel Loveland.

Above:

Exterior view of Strawberry Vale Elementary School, Victoria, British Columbia, designed by Patkau Architects, 1996. Photo: James Dow.

Strawberry Vale School library. Photo: Joel Loveland.

designing with daylight in particular, contributes to our sense both of place and of who we are. We feel that these works offer examples of daylight-responsive architecture that creates interior spaces for work and play and represent a living and continuous reflection of the time, place, and landscape in which they reside.

Water Pollution Control Laboratory, Portland, Oregon, designed by the Miller Hull Partnership and completed in 1997. Photo: The Miller Hull Partnership.

Projects

1

"The best measure of success for us is that the owners are extremely happy with the building and they have actually had employees decline promotions because they did not want to leave the building."
—Scott Wolf, The Miller Hull Partnership

THE MILLER HULL PARTNERSHIP. PROJECT LOCATION: UNIVERSITY PLACE, WASHINGTON

Pierce County Environmental Services Building

Public entry from east parking area.
Photo: C. Meek and K. Van Den Wymelenberg.

Diffuse daylight from overhead skylights
washes the vertical surface of concrete shear
cores at interior open-plan office areas. Photo:
C. Meek and K. Van Den Wymelenberg.

Pierce County Environmental Services Building
1 Open Office
2 Office/Copy Rooms
3 Lobby
4 Public Meeting Room
5 Meeting Room

N⟶

View to the west from covered outdoor area and rain garden. Photo: C. Meek and K. Van Den Wymelenberg.

THE MILLER HULL PARTNERSHIP DESIGNED THE PIERCE COUNTY ENVIRONmental Services Building in direct response to its site context. It is a building fundamentally engaged with the natural landscape, views, and patterns of climate in the coastal Pacific Northwest. The interior spaces are sheltered from the elements but feel much like outdoor places, with prominent views to some of the Northwest's most iconic landforms. The building is anchored at the edge of a bluff overlooking Puget Sound, with the Olympic Mountains to the west and Mount Rainier to the east. Scott Wolf, principal at the Miller Hull Partnership, noted, "Because of the orientation of the bluff and the predominant views to the Sound being due west and Mount Rainier being due east, we made a decision to run the building north-south, which is exactly the wrong way to orient a building for natural light." The designers acknowledged that they were creating a problem from a daylighting standpoint but also determined that the reasons for their decision were too compelling to do otherwise. The opportunity to provide building inhabitants with a powerful visual connection to the surrounding landscape formed one of the primary aspects of the design.

This building breaks perhaps the foremost rule of daylighting planning: elongate the building in the east-west direction. However, daylighting design, and design in general, cannot be reduced to a series of immutable rules. A well-designed building must participate with the specifics of its context. In this case, the site is rooted deep in the cultural mythology of the Pacific Northwest landscape, at the juxtaposition of volcano and sound, mountains and sea. Suppressing that context would have meant furthering the rift between people and place. The designers responded with innovative concepts that provide effective daylighting with comfortable views and a highly energy-efficient building.

BUILDING ORGANIZATION

"The tail of the building is conceived of as a glass box with pods that slash through and are staggered to allow diagonal views through the building."
—Scott Wolf, The Miller Hull Partnership

After the architects decided to shape the building around expansive east and west views, the massing was then divided into public and private areas. The public zone is roughly one-third of the plan and is composed primarily of double-height spaces. It includes the lobby, large meeting rooms, public education areas, and space for other service functions. The private zone, where most of the employees work, is roughly two-thirds of the plan and comprises two floor plates of open office spaces, a small number of private offices, and support spaces such as copy and supply rooms. According to Wolf, the design team "did not want to create a situation in which the senior-level employees had the views and everyone else was excluded."

STRUCTURE, LIGHT, AND AIR

The open floor plan in the office area is structurally supported by a series of concrete shear cores. These rectangular cores run in the east-west direction and are roughly thirty feet long and ten feet wide. They extend from the ground through and above the roof enclosure and enclose private offices, copy rooms, conference rooms, and mechanical space. They alternate on either side of a central corridor running the length of the open-plan office space and create diagonal-view corridors so that each workstation

Public entrance lobby with skylight, translucent baffles, and view to bluff over Puget Sound.
Photo: C. Meek and K. Van Den Wymelenberg.

is never more than thirty feet from a window. The second-floor plate pulls away from the continuous concrete wall of each shear core to reveal a large overhead lightwell that spills light down to the first floor. Each lightwell is capped with a roof monitor designed to provide a daylight and ventilation pathway for both floors. The daylighting concept is not a discrete feature but is fundamentally integrated with the building structure, spatial layout, building organization, and ventilation pathways.

The building uses lightwells to provide daylight primarily from above. This source of diffuse daylight delivers constancy of illumination in contrast to the highly variable illumination from the east- and west-facing glass and provides daylight even when the blinds at the perimeter are deployed. The south clerestory glass and the horizontal skylights have transparent glazing, while the east and west sides of the monitor are translucent. The clear glass allows direct sunlight into the top of the volume, which helps drive stack ventilation by heating the mass of the concrete shear core wall. Concerns about glare from direct sun reflecting off the concrete wall informed the design of a geometric shading system that keeps sunlight out of the occupied spaces. A series of translucent structural panels with intermediate sailcloth baffles suspended between them responds to solar geometry, eliminating nearly all direct sunlight from the office workstations. This baffle system was designed to block direct sunlight without impeding the diffuse light of the overcast sky, which is greatest at the zenith of the sky. It also allows unrestricted airflow for the stack ventilation design.

Diffusing baffles control direct sunlight in the open office while allowing diffuse light from the overcast sky. Photo: C. Meek and K. Van Den Wymelenberg.

A twenty-foot-deep horizontal overhang provides a covered outdoor area and shades the building from direct sunlight until almost four in the afternoon. Photo: C. Meek and K. Van Den Wymelenberg.

Landscape and vegetation at east elevation. Photo: C. Meek and K. Van Den Wymelenberg.

A combination of vegetation and horizontal metal-grate sunshades controls low-angle morning sunlight from the east. Photo: C. Meek and K. Van Den Wymelenberg.

Poplars planted in tight rows act as vertical shading fins and control low-angle morning sunlight. Photo: C. Meek and K. Van Den Wymelenberg.

SHADING THE FAÇADE

Shading the building for glare control and thermal load reduction at the east- and west-facing glazing was extremely challenging, yet it was crucial to occupant comfort and building energy performance. "We worked with the [Seattle Daylighting] Lab on some daylighting models in order to minimize the glare problems created by the orientation," said Scott Wolf. A rule of thumb for shading a south-facing window in the Pacific Northwest is to size the shading device as deep as the window is tall, or a 1:1 ratio. This rule eliminates sunlight during the hottest part of the year, roughly June 21 through September 21, in much of the Pacific Northwest. A west-facing window often requires a different approach; however, due to several compounding factors in this case, the same rule provides adequate sun control. At the Environmental Services Building, the designers followed this guideline and designed a very large twenty-foot roof overhang at the west facade. When including the extra hour of clock time (vs. solar time) during daylight saving time, the warmest times of the year, direct sun does not breach the west facade until after one in the afternoon. Plus, during the times of year that skies are likely to be clear in western Washington (June through September), the sun remains at a high altitude angle, even in the west, until late in the day. In addition, the atypical peak use time for this facility is in the morning hours, with typical occupancy from approximately seven in the morning until three or four in the afternoon. This essentially means that the horizontal overhang, designed at roughly a 1:1 ratio with the west-facing glazing, keeps most of the direct sun out of the space during the vast majority of occupied hours.

This shading element solves more than just glare concerns. In a gesture commensurate with the scale of the site and slope, the deep western overhang shelters outdoor seating and meeting areas adjacent to the building. The approach is ultimately more successful than a series of vertical fins at minimizing glare and solar gain and enables unobstructed access to views of Puget Sound and the Olympic Mountains.

The designers approached the east facade differently. The shift between clock time and solar time during daylight saving time, which helped minimize glare problems on the west facade, adds to the challenge on the east side. Because of adjacent forestland, the view to Mount Rainier in the distance is less compelling than the view to nearby Puget Sound, so the designers were concerned that users would be less likely to reopen blinds after a period of glare. This could have reduced the daylight availability that is crucial to the project's energy-efficiency goals. Therefore, they developed a multifaceted shading approach. Wolf noted, "[Daylight] modeling showed that the east side was actually the more problematic side from a glare standpoint. That led us to develop a series of metal sunscreens that ran up the facade." Additionally, the designers chose to continue the structural bay with dense rows of fast-growing narrow poplars that preserve views toward Mount Rainier while acting as large-scale vertical louvers against low-angle sunlight. Beyond this, three horizontal shading elements are spaced vertically within the two office floor plates and a larger overhang follows the roofline. "We probably would not have had either [strategy] without working with the [Seattle Daylighting] Lab," said Wolf. The combination of landscape and fixed architectural elements substantially reduced, but did not eliminate, the presence of direct sunlight. A roll-down, high-opacity, dark fabric shade was selected to give occupants the ability to control sunlight during periods of extreme glare while preserving some visual access to the outdoors. This combination of approaches has proved successful, given the complexity and dynamic nature of the challenge.

A twenty-foot-deep horizontal overhang controls glare while allowing views to the Olympic Mountains and Puget Sound. Skylights wash interior walls with diffuse daylight from above. Photo: C. Meek and K. Van Den Wymelenberg.

The southernmost open-plan office area receives daylight from three sides. Photo: C. Meek and K. Van Den Wymelenberg.

VISUAL COMFORT AND THE LANDSCAPE

A compelling view improves occupants' perception of visual comfort. The Environmental Services Building can be said to extend the landscape. The design accomplishes this through diffuse daylight and carefully framed vistas. It restores and renews the relationship between the man-made and the natural, with light and views playing a central role in narrating this dialogue. The architects worked to enhance the sense of visual comfort by providing both high-quality daylight and a glare-free working environment inside the building. Interior finishes further these goals. Ultra-bright white ceilings reflect the daylight and improve perceptions of brightness. Office partitions are designed to allow for views and daylight penetration while providing visual and acoustic privacy. Daylight from two, three, and sometimes more directions in a given space conspires to balance the brightness that might occur from low-angle sun through east or west perimeter windows.

This building is a quintessential example of site-responsive architecture in the Cascade region of the Pacific Northwest. It embraces the surrounding outdoor elements and sky conditions to create a space in which occupants maintain a connection to the landscape beyond.

AWARDS

» American Institute of Architects (AIA) Committee on the Environment (COTE), Top Ten Green Projects, 2004
» AIA Washington Council Civic Design Merit Award, 2003

"The abstract qualities of the galleries create a world where only the art exists."

—Jim Olson, Olson Kundig Architects

OLSON KUNDIG ARCHITECTS. PROJECT LOCATION: SEATTLE, WASHINGTON

Wright Exhibition Space

Exterior from Dexter Avenue. Photo: C. Meek.

The darkness of the entry lobby and reception area allows visitors' eyes to adjust to very low light levels. Photo: C. Meek.

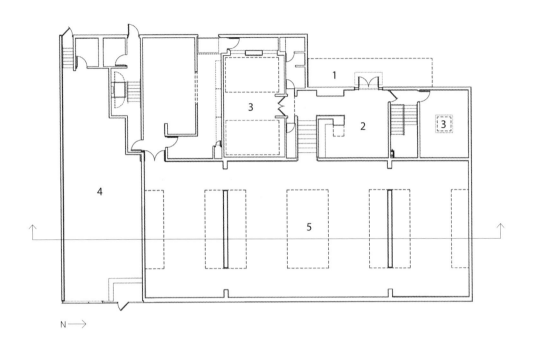

Wright Exhibition Space
1 Entrance Canpoy
2 Entry
3 Private Office
4 Storage
5 Gallery

N⟶

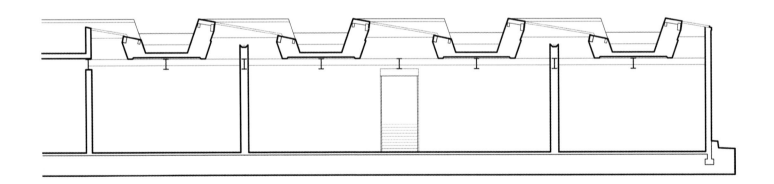

THE WRIGHT EXHIBITION SPACE SERVES AS THE OFFICES AND GALLERY FOR Bagley and Virginia Wright, noted Seattle art collectors and philanthropists. The space was constructed in 1999 and designed by Jim Olson, FAIA, of Olson Kundig Architects. Olson is recognized internationally for his work designing private houses for serious art collectors and for a career that explores "the aesthetic interplay of art and architecture, and the relationship of light, space and mood."[1]

The exhibition space is something of a hidden gem. The single-story concrete block structure sits on an unremarkable site between traffic-choked Aurora Avenue and a decades-old Hostess Cake bakery. The space is open to the public for just a few hours per week. The unassuming street frontage on Dexter Avenue presents no indication of the galleries within. The single clue to their presence is a set of elegant stainless steel numerals placed at the corner of a wall where the ivy has been cut back to reveal the building's address. Visitors access the gallery by first progressing through the alley to the back side of the structure, then moving under a deep, steel canopy awning. The awning, placed above a pair of heavy, hand-crafted, dark bronze doors, immediately begins to reduce the visual brightness and sets up a carefully orchestrated sequence that transports a visitor from the everyday world to a space that creates a spare yet dynamic setting for one of the world's foremost contemporary art collections.

SEQUENCE OF DAYLIGHT AND SPACE

Upon entering the building, the perception of darkness is immediate and complete. After a pause, as eyes adjust to the sudden compression, the edges of the space reveal themselves. Rich, chocolate brown walls, a red-orange–hued painting, a thin glass sculpture, and a small seating area emerge from the darkness. A single skylight casts a blue glow at a reception desk in the corner where the Wrights' assistant works. The combina-

An entrance canopy of dark wood reduces brightness upon approach to the gallery entrance. Photo: C. Meek.

High-contrast translucent art-glass windows and electric light sources with dark interior surface finishes reinforce the perception of darkness. Photo: C. Meek.

Stair to exhibition space. Photo: C. Meek.

The central gallery at the Wright Exhibition Space opens to the sky with white walls and diffusing skylights. Photo: C. Meek.

tion of the dark surface finishes and the intensity of the tiny spotlights that highlight the color and depth of the artwork drives the eye to adjust to a very low level of luminosity. A pair of translucent hand-made art-glass windows on each side of the entry door increases the sense of darkness by introducing subtle hints of the brightness just outside.

To the right is the faint glow of Bagley Wright's office, reconstructed on-site in great detail after being carefully dismantled and relocated from its previous location in a downtown Seattle high-rise. Proceeding toward the office, visitors come across a gradual ramping stair to an stunningly white room and pale gray floor. As they continue down the stair and enter the gallery, the artwork within comes into immediate focus. The space, finished entirely with white walls and ceiling, exudes light yet does not insert itself between the viewer and the artwork. "The abstract qualities of the galleries create a world where only the art exists," observes Olson, noting the inward focus of the gallery spaces. However, this is not an isolated and static interior environment. The presence of the sky beyond the gallery and the subtle changes in intensity and color it engenders have a profound impact on the space.

During the design stage, the architects developed several aperture and skylight well schemes including vertical monitors, transparent north-facing clerestories, and horizontal skylights, which were tested to assess the distribution of light on the interior walls of the galleries. In direct response to the nature of Seattle's overcast, the designers selected diffuse horizontal apertures that open to the zenith of the sky and directly engage the vertical surfaces of each gallery. This relationship between light source and surface provides consistent illumination across changing sky conditions and cre-

A diffuse skylight washes both sides of a gallery wall with diffuse daylight. Photo: C. Meek.

South gallery space. Photo: C. Meek.

Diffuse daylight apertures engage vertical surfaces, creating a series of illuminated planes.
Photo: C. Meek.

Central gallery space looking south.
Photo: C. Meek.

ates a quality of light that reveals the walls of each gallery and the work displayed within. Visitors experience the space through a receding series of diffuse planes of pure light that act as a foil to the pieces of art. Walls centered on the skylights allow light to cascade down both sides, which become the primary source of illumination for the galleries. The designers chose the pale concrete floor and whitewashed wood-plank ceiling to provide textural and material relief within the space. Yet these materials maintain an ethereal presence while greatly increasing the inter-reflectance of light. Though the artwork speaks for itself, the physical space created for its display creates a sense of mystery and discovery. Whereas many works of contemporary architecture strive to convey their form and function through immediate legibility, the Wright Exhibition Space unfolds slowly, promising nothing, yet offering an experience of light and space that speaks to the aspirations and values of Pacific Northwest culture.

3

"We didn't just want to meet a LEED [Leadership in Energy and Environmental Design] requirement or have a marginal amount of daylight but were eager to have every space work without turning on the electric lights during daylight hours."

—Rich Franko, Mithun

MITHUN. PROJECT LOCATION: SEATTLE, WASHINGTON

Yesler Way Community Center

Entry from Yesler Avenue.
Photo: C. Meek and K. Van Den Wymelenberg.

Gymnasium under overcast skies.
Photo: C. Meek and K. Van Den Wymelenberg.

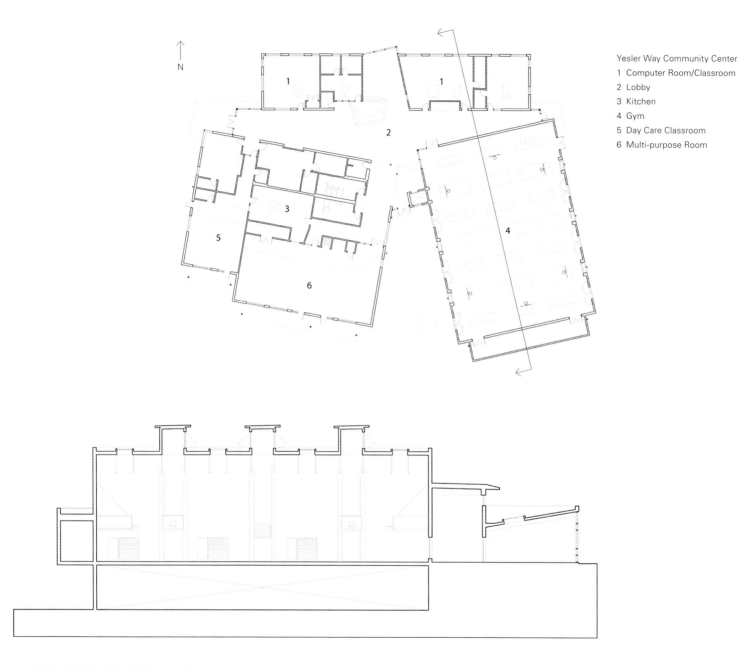

Yesler Way Community Center
1 Computer Room/Classroom
2 Lobby
3 Kitchen
4 Gym
5 Day Care Classroom
6 Multi-purpose Room

THE DAYLIGHTING DESIGN AT THE YESLER WAY COMMUNITY CENTER IS THE product of a collaborative partnership between Mithun, Keen Engineering (now Stantec Engineering), and the Seattle Daylighting Lab, where the concept of a daylit and naturally ventilated gymnasium was reenvisioned.

The building was commissioned in 2001 shortly after former Seattle mayor Paul Schell mandated that all public construction be built to the U.S. Green Building Council's LEED Silver standard. Mithun, with a national reputation for designing toward sustainability, assembled a building delivery team that would set a new standard for the Seattle Parks Department. While Seattle's mayor provided leadership in promoting green building on a regional scale, the Seattle Parks Department would require some convincing.

Beginning with a blank slate makes for a challenge. The design team engaged in an academic approach that critically investigated all the major design elements that would have an impact on user comfort and energy use. The architects set a goal of delivering a building that could function without electric lights during daylight hours and was ventilated and cooled naturally, without refrigeration. With these ambitious goals, they undertook a set of daylight and airflow analyses that served to develop and refine the form of the building. The architectural geometry began to resolve after months of iterative physical and digital daylight modeling as well as airflow and computation fluid dynamics modeling. The design team analyzed extensive variations of view windows, skylights, clerestories, roof monitors, damper vents, and inlets and outlets for their effects on visual comfort, thermal comfort, and energy performance. Rich Franko, lead designer at Mithun, stated, "Our key concepts of natural ventilation and daylighting worked very well together." These parametric variations were studied further at a more refined level after preliminary, conceptual investigations. Aspect ratios, relative size, operable capabilities, and material properties such as transparency, translucency, and thermal characteristics were optimized around predefined energy and daylighting design goals.

Horizontal translucent skylights, left, optimized for daylight and vertical glass monitors, right, optimized for passive cooling. Photo: C. Meek and K. Van Den Wymelenberg.

SITE GEOMETRY AND BUILDING ORGANIZATION

The site slopes downward to the south and carries an impressive view toward downtown Seattle and Mount Rainier. Viewed from the street side at the north edge of the property, the building sits within a mixed-income residential neighborhood. In a direct engagement of the street, the sidewalk along the exterior continues inside the building, becoming an interior street, with the major activity spaces available on each side. The interior street draws the sensibilities of the exterior urban environment into the community center while establishing a clear interior presence. This space is daylit by clerestory windows to the north and south and is finished with a polished concrete floor and an exposed metal deck ceiling. Its raw industrial finishes and dramatic patterns of light and dark set it apart from the visually warmer, more uniformly illuminated rooms to which it affords access. The motorized north- and south-facing clerestory windows operate to provide natural cross-ventilation and space cooling.

The remainder of the building program consists of a gym, a multipurpose dance room, classrooms, digital media rooms, a kitchen, staff offices, and a day-care facility. A large multipurpose space and the day-care classrooms are accessed from the south side of the interior street and benefit from the expansive view to the south. The teen center and computer lab are accessed directly from the north side of the interior street. These digital-media-dominated spaces are subject to more stringent visual comfort and direct-sun control criteria. They therefore require lower light levels and thus are located where they receive diffused northern light. Storefront windows open to a canopy of trees at the north sidewalk and provide a

View to daylit gymnasium from interior street.
Photo: C. Meek and K. Van Den Wymelenberg.

Interior street with operable clerestory
windows for daylight and passive cooling.
Photo: C. Meek and K. Van Den Wymelenberg.

View from gymnasium to interior street.
Photo: C. Meek and K. Van Den Wymelenberg.

Day care classroom looking south.
Photo: C. Meek and K. Van Den Wymelenberg.

Operable skylights illuminate the back of the game room while providing a path for passive ventilation. Photo: C. Meek and K. Van Den Wymelenberg.

visual connection to the adjacent street while welcoming the community into the center. Transparent south-facing skylights introduce dynamic daylight into the space near the innermost wall and allow for natural ventilation exhaust when necessary. The skylight well depth limits the presence of direct southern sunlight.

GYMNASIUM

Elevated above a small parking area, the gymnasium anchors the building on the sloping site and occupies the east edge of the complex. Although the gym is elongated in the north-south direction, low-angle direct sunlight from the east and west is not a concern because daylight is introduced solely from above, through eight alternating roof monitors composed of different combinations of north-facing transparent glass, south-facing translucent glass, and translucent skylights. Open-web steel joists span a concrete block structure with roof monitors that represent nearly 50 percent of the total roof area. Specifically, four roof monitors built with south-facing translucent skylights that are optimized around daylight performance alternate with four roof monitors composed of south-facing translucent vertical glazing and north-facing operable, clear vertical glazing designed primarily as ventilation apertures. Performance criteria included providing functional illumination during all daylight hours while keeping direct-beam sunlight out of the space during occupied times in order to limit solar gain and control glare. The ventilation and cooling strategy was developed in tandem with the daylighting design, with each informing and modulating the demands of the other. In particular, the amount of south-facing glazing, necessary for good daylight uniformity in the space, was carefully sized relative to the ventilation potential of the north-facing operable clerestories. The design omitted perimeter view windows for programmatic reasons and in an effort to minimize glare. Further, the carefully tested matte finish specified for the wood flooring softens direct reflections from all light sources, including daylight.

The surface-mounted linear fluorescent lighting system and the daylight apertures were coordinated by location and, controlled by photocells, respond to the presence of daylight. The gymnasium is so well daylit that electric lighting is necessary only at night and on very dark days. The Seattle Parks Department was so pleased with the outcome that daylight has become a standard feature of all new gymnasiums it commissions.

MULTIPURPOSE ROOM

The multipurpose room serves as a community meeting room and a dance studio. Raw exposed materials compose the aesthetic of the whole building, which carries through to the multipurpose room in the form of exposed, open-web, metal-web wood joists that support a plywood roof deck. A hardwood dance floor mirrors the wood ceiling. This amount of exposed wood, even though specified with high reflectance, posed a challenge to the goal of meeting more than half of the illumination requirements for this space through daylighting.

The daylighting strategy began with large perimeter windows at the south envelope. A continuous break in the building section allows for north clerestories. The innermost third of the ceiling lifts more than six feet in order to create a large monitor that runs the entire length of the room. Clerestory windows in this roof monitor deliver diffuse north light onto the wall opposite the band of south-view windows. This wall, painted white to reflect the daylight from above, balances the brightness from the perimeter windows. The bright white vertical surfaces, intentionally located to reflect the daylight, combine with light-hued wood tones to produce an effective composition of light and dark.

Meeting the goal of ensuring natural cooling and avoiding glare required solar shading. The roof structure extends over a large exterior viewing patio and shades the expansive south windows. This eliminates unwanted solar heat during the warm months. The patio extends to a railed balcony, provid-

North-facing operable clerestories balance the brightness of south-facing windows in the multipurpose room. Photo: C. Meek and K. Van Den Wymelenberg.

ing a large outdoor gathering space with a tremendous view. The multipurpose room opens onto the patio through several doors, further connecting the interior experience with the surrounding neighborhood.

A NEW STANDARD FOR DESIGN

According to Rich Franko, "This project was groundbreaking for the Seattle Parks Department in terms of overcoming their concerns about glare. The [Seattle] Daylighting Lab was essential in this process." The evidence provided by daylight modeling, visits to effectively daylit gyms, and a growing consensus around the need for more energy-efficient buildings led the Seattle Parks Department to consider deviating from long-held standards against skylights in its facilities, which had previously precluded effective daylighting design in gymnasiums. The project team's integrated design process led to a building that realizes new design possibilities for daylit and naturally ventilated architecture in the Pacific Northwest.

AWARDS

» AIA Washington Council Civic Design citation, 2006
» AIA Seattle Committee on the Environment (COTE), "What Makes It Green?" 2005
» USGBC, LEED Gold, 2005

North-facing roof monitors provide daylight
from above in the day-care classroom.
Photo: C. Meek and K. Van Den Wymelenberg.

4

"This building is innovative in the quality of its interior spaces and its forward-thinking relationship to energy use. The quality of daylight in the interior spaces is particularly unique for an office environment and provides flexibility in the case of future energy limitations."
—American Institute of Architects Washington Council jury

WEBER + THOMPSON. PROJECT LOCATION: SEATTLE, WASHINGTON

Terry Thomas Building

Exterior view looking southwest.
Photo: C. Meek and K. Van Den Wymelenberg.

Daylight from two sides, high interior-surface reflectance values, and a narrow floor plate allow for balanced distribution of daylighting throughout the Terry Thomas Building. Photo: C. Meek and K. Van Den Wymelenberg.

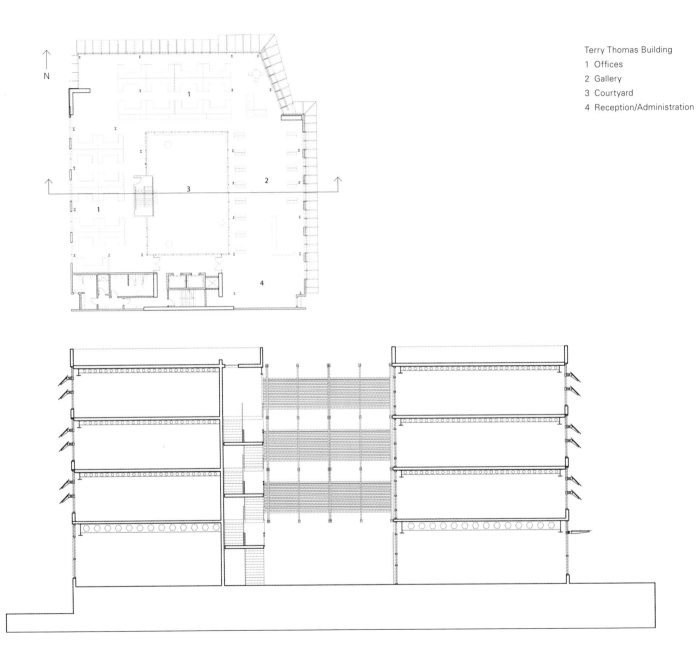

Terry Thomas Building
1 Offices
2 Gallery
3 Courtyard
4 Reception/Administration

WHEN THE PARTNERS AT WEBER + THOMPSON DECIDED TO BUILD A NEW building for their firm, they asked their employees what they most desired in a new office environment. Natural light and fresh air were at the top of the list, so the influence of light and air on the interior spaces became fundamental to the conceptual morphology of the building. "The quality of the indoor environment was of the utmost importance to our employees, as it put their health and well-being at the highest priority. Thermal comfort, daylighting, and fresh air were the most important considerations in the design," explains partner Scott Thompson, AIA.

Daylighting design goals and aspirations can vary widely among building types and the visual tasks they support. However, there is a chain of interrelated design elements that connects the sky and its patterns of illumination at the macro scale with an individual work space and the specific needs of a person who will use that physical setting in accomplishing specific tasks. This set of linkages is complex and includes the site and sky as a light source, the massing and orientation of the building, the depth of the floor plate, the aperture size and location, architectural elements and window coverings, interior surfaces and their luminous properties, interior furnishings including partition layout and design, and, ultimately, the ergonomics of the individual workstation, including the direction in which the occupant faces and the character of the primary visual field and task surfaces. Any daylighting design scheme, especially in an office environment, is only as successful as the weakest component of this crucial set of linkages. The design of the Terry Thomas Building addresses each of these relationships robustly so that the building provides persistent daylight performance to its occupants regardless of sun position or sky conditions across the vast majority of daylight hours.

Interior courtyard with exterior stair.
Photo: C. Meek and K. Van Den Wymelenberg.

MASSING AND SITE

Seattle's dominant sky condition is overcast. Achieving effective daylight illumination in multistory office buildings in this climate requires workstations to be directly adjacent or very close to windows at the perimeter (generally within twenty feet). Historically, as evidenced in the massing of nearly all office buildings built before World War II, this resulted in thin-plan buildings arranged in linear bars, foursquare with windows on two sides, or around courtyards with the section depth limited by the physics of natural light distribution and the movement of air for cross-ventilation. In this strategy, daylight zones were not simply prioritized to the perimeter; the *entire building* was a perimeter zone. Weber + Thompson adopted this strategy as the starting point for its daylighting and passive ventilation design. The Terry Thomas Building, which is organized around a rectangular open courtyard, has a total section depth limited to thirty-eight feet, with the central

courtyard of a similar dimension. This means that no portion of the building, and therefore no workstation, is more than nineteen feet from a window. Creating a narrow floor plate with a courtyard is a design move as simple and straightforward as it is radical in our current commercial office culture. However, rather than guaranteeing successful daylight performance, proper massing and a narrow section depth merely set the stage for the amount and quality of daylight illumination required to support the visual comfort demands of an office environment.

APERTURES

According to the AIA's Committee on the Environment (COTE), the Terry Thomas Building is "Seattle's first major new office building in decades to feature passive cooling. Instead of air conditioning, the 40,000-square-foot building is cooled naturally through a number of design strategies includ-

Third-floor open office looking east with courtyard on right and translucent wall to break room beyond. Photo: C. Meek and K. Van Den Wymelenberg.

Second-floor open-plan office area looking east. Photo: C. Meek and K. Van Den Wymelenberg.

The break room creates a dynamic flexible-use space while shielding office areas from direct sunlight with a translucent wall to the west. Photo: C. Meek and K. Van Den Wymelenberg.

ing operable windows." This design approach meant that the control of solar loads at the building envelope and the reduction of internal heat loads from lighting were crucial to the success of the design. Apertures needed to be large enough to deliver sufficient daylight illumination on overcast days without opening the building up to excessive solar radiation during the warmest months of the year, goals that are at cross-purposes in many ways. Weber + Thompson addressed this challenge by working with the Seattle Daylighting Lab and Tom Marseilles, principal engineer at Stantec Engineering.

This collaboration led to a design that meets both the visual comfort requirements of effective daylighting and the thermal requirements for creating a comfortable, energy-efficient building. Designs for passive solar shading and glare control are related yet distinct activities. Solar shading addresses periods when a building is likely to be in cooling mode, while glare control must be effective during *all* occupied hours. The conflation

of these two design activities frequently results in buildings that never meet their daylight potential. One of the basic tenets of visual comfort is the ability to completely block the line of sight to the disc of the sun at all times. Unfortunately, many commercial buildings deploy blinds nearly permanently in position for the worst-case scenario when they must overcome extreme glare from the disc of the sun, resulting in poor daylight performance and the elimination of views to the exterior. This is especially common in shared work environments where the lowest common denominator of visual comfort rules. Using this as a basis for evaluating design ideas, the design team engaged in thermal and daylight simulation, which enabled it to tune building apertures to solar orientation and create facades modulated by specific shading and glare-control strategies.

At the Terry Thomas Building, east- and west-facing windows are largely punched openings shaded by transparent, spectrally selective glass sunshades designed to keep incident solar radiation below thresholds that would ordinarily trigger the need for refrigeration on warm days. On the east facade, low-angle direct sun would be present and problematic on a daily basis. Therefore, program elements, including break rooms, copy rooms, and flexible-use spaces such as conference rooms, where occupants can adjust blinds to meet specific meeting and audiovisual needs, were located on the east side of the building. Additionally, since these rooms tend to be compact, smaller glazing areas were deemed sufficient for supplying effective illumination.

The open-plan offices to the north, south, and west required larger areas of glazing and a higher level of glare control for persistent visual comfort across the large, shared, open office environments. Window apertures

Exterior automated venetian blinds deploy to control direct sunlight and retract during overcast sky conditions. Photo: C. Meek and K. Van Den Wymelenberg.

Ceiling heights on the ground floor are increased by two feet, enabling sufficient daylight from the bottom of the courtyard and the perimeter glazing. Photo: C. Meek and K. Van Den Wymelenberg.

Diffuse daylight on interior surfaces allows for comfortable views within this gallery area while maintaining minimal contrast with views to the courtyard. Photo: C. Meek and K. Van Den Wymelenberg.

at all perimeter and atrium courtyard zones, with less glass area to the west, achieve daylight performance under overcast skies. This is where the goals of providing sufficient ambient diffuse daylight under overcast skies and blocking all direct sunlight on sunny days come into direct conflict. The design team chose to use exterior automated venetian blinds, a strategy common in northern Europe, to meet both requirements. Though it may seem odd that buildings in cool, cloudy climates would focus such effort on solar shading, there are clear benefits to this strategy. Fixed exterior shading devices such as horizontal sunshades or louvers can substantially reduce the amount of diffuse daylight illumination entering a building on overcast days, requiring increased glass area to meet daylight performance goals and maintain high-quality views. The benefit of exterior automated venetian blinds is that they provide complete solar shading when the sun is out, regardless of sun angle, and retract when clouds are present or the sun is not on a particular facade. This movement is generated through a

photocell on the roof that senses whether the sky is cloudy or clear. Blind deployment and slat angle control are based on an astronomical time clock that is programmed with the sun's path based on the site's latitude and the facade orientation. The exterior blinds enable the Terry Thomas Building to respond directly to climate conditions and ensures optimum daylight performance. The response changes with the patterns of light from the sky, maintains views, and, most important, ensures a comfortable environment for the creative activities the space was designed to support.

INTERIORS

The building geometry, shallow section depth, window area, solar shading, and glare-control systems conspire to provide extensive high-quality daylight illumination to the entire building enclosure. However, without an interior design that makes effective use of that illumination and responds to the distribution of daylight within the interior volume, much of these efforts would be for naught. Weber + Thompson knew that high levels of interior surface reflectance were key to both the perception of brightness and the maximization of the inter-reflection of daylight. White paint and reflective clouds in the upper volume of the space reduce reliance on electric lighting. Beams that run parallel to daylight apertures are castellated in order to avoid shadowing across the ceiling plane. Light-colored interior partitions and low partition heights ensure that deep cavities do not create dark surfaces on workstations and other visual task planes. Many office partitions positioned in parallel to daylight apertures are constructed of transparent glazing and allow daylight penetration while creating a sense of enclosure. Perhaps the most important interior-space planning decision was to keep the open-plan office areas open to the perimeter glazing on two and often three sides. This has a twofold benefit. First, when shading devices are deployed on one side due to direct sunlight on clear days, the opposite side is likely to provide sufficient daylight to make up for the shortfall caused by the closed blinds. Second, the balance of brightness across the section is consistently self-regulated by another source of daylight regardless of the sky condition. When spaces are illuminated from a single side, the excessive contrast nearly always makes the interior wall opposite the windows appear dark during daytime hours.

The design of the workstations allows the primary visual field from most workstations to be parallel to daylight openings. This helps avoid visual discomfort caused by users looking into their own shadows or, worse, the excessive contrast that might occur when a visual task area, such as a computer monitor, is surrounded by the brightness of a view to the exterior.

From the fundamental arrangement of the architecture to the specific task areas of its inhabitants, the design of the Terry Thomas Building reconciles the connection between the sky and climate with the visual requirements of its inhabitants. It is only through a holistic view of the crucial interrelationships between site, massing, apertures, solar control, interior surfaces, and individual work spaces that daylight can serve as the primary source of functional illumination in offices. The Terry Thomas Building advances a model for a daylit, energy-efficient, urban office building by combining traditional architectural form with contemporary technology and meets a complex design context with resilience and functionality.

AWARDS

» AIA Committee on the Environment (COTE) Top Ten Green Projects, 2009
» American Society of Interior Designers (ASID) Northwest Design Award, 2009
» Excellence in Construction Award, Sustainable Building Category, by the Associated Builders & Contractors of Western Washington, 2009
» Northwest and Pacific Region AIA Honor Award, 2009
» Sustainable Development of the Year by the National Association of Industrial and Office Properties (NAIOP) Washington State Chapter, 2009
» AIA Seattle Honor Awards, 2008
» *Eco-Structure Magazine*'s Evergreen Award, 2008
» U.S. Green Building Council (USGBC), LEED Gold, 2008
» USGBC, LEED Platinum, 2008

5

"The early concepts for the planning of the Morse Center focused on optimizing daylighting in the welding and auto repair technology lab spaces. Typically, these spaces rely heavily on artificial light, and inhabitants can spend hours without the relief of natural light or an awareness of the outside world."

—Julie Blazek, HKP Architects

HKP ARCHITECTS. PROJECT LOCATION: BELLINGHAM, WASHINGTON

Bellingham Technical College David & Joyce Morse Center

Exterior looking north.
Photo: C. Meek and C. Von Rueden.

Metal shop with diffuse skylights and view to shop yard. Photo: C. Meek and C. Von Rueden.

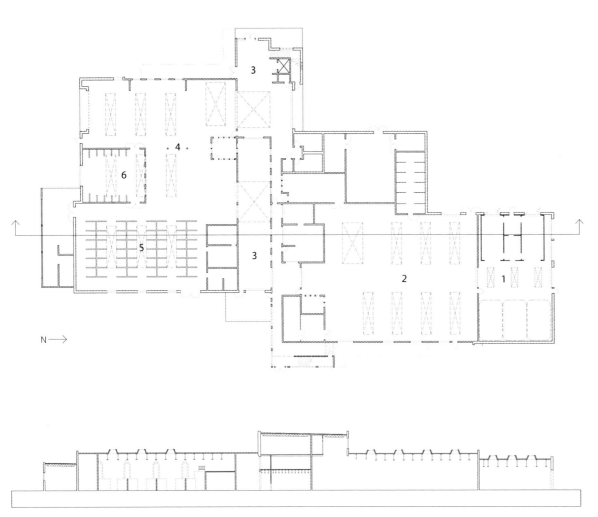

David & Joyce Morse Center
at Bellingham Technical College
1 Paint and Body Shop
2 Auto Technology
3 Entry
4 Metal Shop
5 Arc Welding Shop
6 Welding Shop

N⟶

THERE IS A LONG HISTORY OF THE USE OF DAYLIGHT IN INDUSTRIAL FACILI-
ties. From the outset of the industrial revolution until the middle of the
twentieth century, the optimism fueled by the dawn of the golden age
of American manufacturing was manifest in the great cathedrals of light
designed by architects such as Albert Kahn. These bold designs arose
from functional necessity. Great halls for manufacturing were designed to
provide functional daylight illumination from sunrise to sundown because
primitive electric lighting systems could not supply the levels or quality of
illumination deemed necessary for performing visual tasks of ever-increas-
ing complexity on a grand scale. As the electric lighting industry developed
high-bay luminaire technology using fluorescent and metal-halide lamps,
electric lighting took over the role of providing consistent, dependable illumination, and, subsequently, many architects ceded their role in designing
the luminous environment. With the Morse Center at Bellingham Technical College, HKP Architects breathes life back into industrial work-space
design with a carefully crafted toplighting configuration that is efficient and
utilitarian yet recognizes that the best architecture is about the drama of
spatial surfaces in light.

The David & Joyce Morse Center sits at the core of the welding, metal
fabrication, and auto technology education and training program at Bellingham Technical College. As Julie Blazek, partner at HKP Architects,
explains, "The early concepts for the planning of the Morse Center focused
on optimizing daylighting in the welding and auto repair technology lab
spaces. Typically, these spaces rely heavily on artificial light, and inhabitants can spend hours without the relief of natural light or an awareness of
the outside world." The goal for this project was to create an environment
that recognized the nature of the work and supported it with appropriate

Diffuse daylight washes vertical surfaces and
provides functional illumination at fume hoods.
Photo: C. Meek and C. Von Rueden.

illumination while enabling occupants to connect to the outdoors and the temporal variability of daylight.

SHOP FLOOR AND YARD

The metal shop floor provides for clear span open space and large gantry cranes as required for metalworking at all scales. In a single-story high-bay space with a large floor plate, the only viable daylighting option is to illuminate the space from above. The toplighting design of the open shop area is crafted to provide diffuse horizontal illumination across the entire floor plate so as to functionally illuminate shop activities under both overcast and clear skies. It achieves this with large, translucent-panel skylights that are engineered to deliver an appropriate range of illumination based on a direct relationship between the floor area of the shop, the visible-light transmission of the panel, the size and position of the apertures, and the patterns

Pipes, conduit, and ceiling structure are painted white, enhancing daylight reflection and increasing the perception of brightness. Photo: C. Meek and C. Von Rueden.

Daylit welding booth with task light. Photo: C. Meek and C. Von Rueden.

Transparent clerestories add sparkle to the artwork *Those things that are too small to see will soon become too large to ignore*, by Kim David Hall. Photo: C. Meek and C. Von Rueden.

In the auto technology bays, a light-surfaced concrete floor helps inter-reflect daylight from overhead skylights as do the reflective wall panels used for noise reduction. Photo: C. Meek and C. Von Rueden.

of available daylight in western Washington. The translucent panels block all direct sun while creating an even distribution of light within the volume. Because of these design decisions, the shop frequently operates with the electric lights off for the entire day. As Blazek notes, "Many of the spaces operate during school hours without the assistance of general or task lighting. Perhaps the most noticeable feature of the building is the overall balance of the light, even moving from the exterior into the building."

Diffuse skylight illuminates the space between the painting and auto body workshops, while transparent overhead doors provide a view to the exterior. Photo: C. Meek and C. Von Rueden.

Although the design's primary consideration was to achieve sufficient light levels at critical task surfaces, the surrounding surfaces were not neglected. The concrete floor was left unfinished with a high reflectance value in order to ensure maximum light inter-reflection back to the ceiling surface and structure, which were painted white. Skylights placed at the perimeter of the shop wash the walls with daylight. This strategy helps define the extent of the architectural volume and creates a sense of brightness throughout the space.

WELDING BOOTHS

Programmatic demands required the installation of dozens of partitioned welding cubicles that would ensure a safe working environment for students. This could have easily prevented the inclusion of daylight for a large portion of the educational spaces. However, the design team felt that the goal of including functional daylight for all students was paramount. The team designed concrete-block welding booths that are open to the high bay ceiling above, facilitating the passage of light and air. After careful simulation and testing of multiple design options, the team placed translucent skylights that deliver diffuse light to each booth with minimal shadowing. The extensive service pipes, ventilation ducts, and conduits required to support the welding rigs are painted white in the upper volume of the space, allowing for light inter-reflection and avoiding the dark shadows and extensive cavities that would curtail daylight performance. High-quality task-level illumination is provided during nearly all daylight hours to what might have been one of the most isolated locations of the building.

AUTOMOTIVE TECHNOLOGY SPACES

The automotive technology classrooms continue the strategy of using translucent horizontal skylights to provide diffuse daylight illumination. Addi-

tionally, rectangular acoustic panels on the interior wall surface enhance light inter-reflection and improve the acoustic performance of the space. Although diffuse toplighting is the dominant daylighting strategy, expansive glass garage doors facilitate the movement of vehicles into and out of the shop and provide views to the adjacent campus landscape. The only elements of the program that are not fundamentally daylit are the painting and abrasive bodywork bays. The decision to exclude daylight from these areas was driven by prioritization and functional requirements. Both space types are intermittently occupied. Therefore, they were given a lower priority for daylight than the high-occupancy spaces. Beyond this, both space types require special air-quality control. The painting bays must be isolated from any airborne particulate matter, while the abrasive bodywork bays produce extensive debris that must be excluded from the rest of the building. For these reasons, the design team determined that the inclusion of skylights was impractical in these areas. However, it should be noted that visual access to the larger daylit area is an integral part of the design of these spaces.

Diffuse daylight is most appropriate for the visual tasks performed within the building. For this reason, most glazing that was not designed specifically to afford a view is translucent. However, transparent clerestories were included in a roof monitor specifically designed to showcase a large-scale, suspended, pulled-polymer sculpture by Seattle artist Kim David Hall. The clerestories allow controlled direct sunlight to illuminate the deformed polymer and animate the space with unpredictable patterns of refracted light. This design element provides an area of focus and idiosyncrasy in an otherwise highly uniform space.

6

"The lesson for me was to pay a lot of attention to the balance of the light."
—Craig Curtis, The Miller Hull Partnership

THE MILLER HULL PARTNERSHIP. PROJECT LOCATION: PORT ORCHARD, WASHINGTON

Kitsap County Administration Building

The main entrance canopy pulls away from a concrete wall, allowing daylight to wash the surface. Photo: C. Meek and K. Van Den Wymelenberg.

Skylights supplement vertical windows to provide diffuse daylight across this thirty-six-foot-deep open-office floor plate. Photo: C. Meek and K. Van Den Wymelenberg.

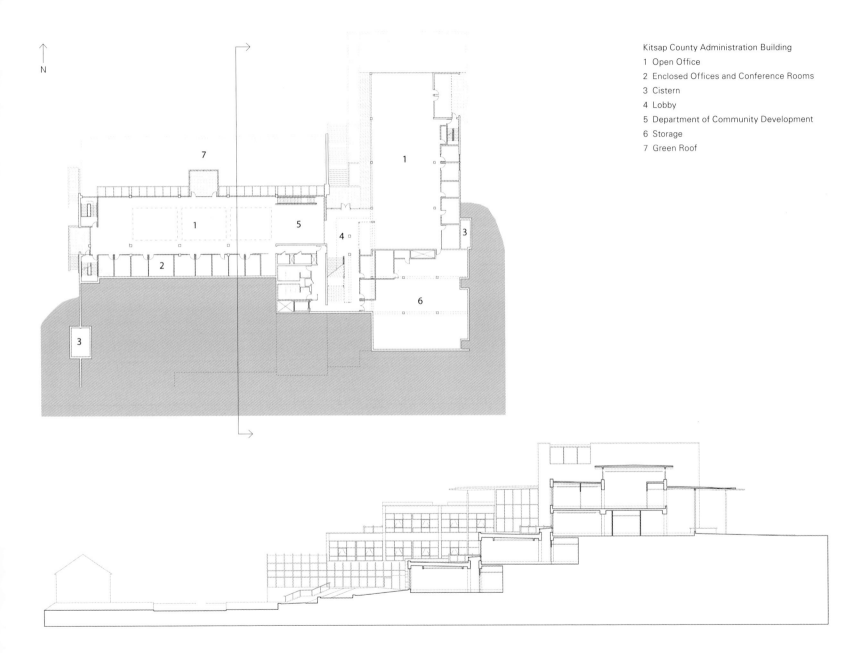

Kitsap County Administration Building
1 Open Office
2 Enclosed Offices and Conference Rooms
3 Cistern
4 Lobby
5 Department of Community Development
6 Storage
7 Green Roof

THE KITSAP COUNTY ADMINISTRATION BUILDING SITS HIGH ABOVE PUGET Sound on a steep hillside overlooking Sinclair Inlet and Bremerton Harbor to the north. When the Miller Hull Partnership was asked to consolidate several county departmental offices into a new 70,000-square-foot office building on the site, while incorporating a stunning fifty-five-foot grade change, the design team knew it had a remarkable opportunity. One of the project's many successes is that it takes the best attributes of the site and shares them generously and equitably among building users. Foremost among these shared attributes are the light and landscape of the Puget Sound region. A comment from the building's facilities director tells the story succinctly: "It is probably the one thing mentioned more often than anything else when you ask the staff how they like working there—it's the light." Craig Curtis, partner-in-charge at Miller Hull and resident of Kitsap County, happened to be serving jury duty directly across from the site in the early days of schematic design. "At lunch I would just sit and stare at the site, and immediately I was interested in the idea of terracing the building into the hillside, keeping the floor plates very narrow to get light into them, stacking the floors until you can make up the grade change, and you can open up the building on both sides." This early vision of a terraced building imbued with daylight proved to be the primary driver of the design.

BUILDING MASSING

All of the office floor plates face north, except for a select few at the top of the site that open to both the north and the south. Low-angle morn-

Daylight through a ceiling slot skylight illuminates this public lobby and café. Vertical windows frame views to Puget Sound to the south. Photo: C. Meek and K. Van Den Wymelenberg.

ing sunlight is blocked by a grove of mature trees to the east. The building forms a monumental staircase with the functional program elements woven through it while expressing the steep slope of the site. This open stair provides access to public portions of the building, including the council chambers, meeting rooms, and reception areas of the county's public service departments.

COMMISSIONERS' AND SUPPORT STAFF OFFICES

The Kitsap County commissioners' offices occupy the highest point of the building at the perimeter zone overlooking Sinclair Inlet to the north. In most cases, the location of individual offices at the perimeter would leave the windowless "cubicle farms" of the in-board spaces unrelieved by the light of day or views to the exterior. These offices are far different. On this top floor, well above grade level, high clerestory windows bring in light from two sides at the in-board shared office spaces, circumventing many of the issues associated with perimeter private offices. Since the building faces directly north, there is no need for shading or blinds at the north-facing clerestory. The south clerestory is another matter. Horizontal exterior sunshades block southern sunlight during months when the building is likely to be in cooling mode; however, low-angle sunlight could potentially sneak

Top floor open office looking east. Clerestories illuminate this interior open-plan office area while the massing of the copy and break room (at right) blocks direct sun from the southern clerestories. Photo: C. Meek and K. Van Den Wymelenberg.

Top-floor open-plan office area looking through commissioners' offices to views of Sinclair Inlet. Photo: C. Meek and K. Van Den Wymelenberg.

North-facing windows and green roof at stepped open offices. Note skylight at left to offices below. Photo: C. Meek and K. Van Den Wymelenberg.

through and cause debilitating glare during occasional sunny winter days. Thoughtful space planning mitigated this concern. Support spaces, including a break room, a copy room, and conference rooms, were located to the south side of the office, with a hard-lid ceiling at twelve feet that acts as an interior lightshelf; this shields occupants from harsh direct sunlight entering from the clerestory windows above, diffusing and redirecting the light to reflective ceiling clouds. Recalling the process of working with the Seattle Daylighting Lab, Curtis remarks, "It was a tough one for me architecturally [the clerestory in the top-floor offices], but when you go up there now, without that clerestory, it would not have been nearly as good. That was purely the result of the daylighting study."

Similar care was taken in providing equity of views to the support staff. The sweeping views from the commissioners' offices are shared with the rest of the floor through all-glass partition walls placed between the private offices and the central open office space. Similarly, there are no blinds to obscure this spatial relationship. Since the commissioners tend to spend the majority of their time in the field meeting with constituents, this arrangement ensures that all occupants realize the benefits of the views throughout the day and year.

COUNTY DEPARTMENT OFFICE FLOORS

The county's departmental offices are terraced down the hillside, partially embedded in the earth and opening to the sweeping northern views of the waterway below and the Olympic Mountains beyond. Large windows showcase the panorama while providing daylight to about half of the open-office floor plate along the perimeter wall. A transparent strip of skylights washes the back wall with daylight and offers unobstructed views to the sky overhead, balancing the daylight in the space and illuminating the interior half of the floor plate. Ordinarily, transparent glass would create serious problems with direct-beam sunlight and glare in an open office environ-

West facade showing stepped office floors.
Photo: C. Meek and K. Van Den Wymelenberg.

ment. However, due to the terraced mass of the building to the south above each skylight, the transparent openings remain in shadow nearly all of the time. Direct sunlight tracks through the back of the office floor plate only when the sun is perpendicular to the openings in the east or west of the building. Even then, the sunlight is present only for a short time and is always restricted to the circulation way, where visual comfort requirements are much less demanding. In fact, these short periods of solar intensity in the corridor diffuse sunlight within the space, increasing the surface brightness of the walls and ceiling. Other than small punched openings at the termination of the circulation aisle, no glass faces east or west, thereby ensuring visual comfort and balanced lighting.

The cumulative benefit of these design decisions, especially the inclusion of the skylights at the core, is that daylight illumination levels on the interior surfaces are balanced throughout the space. This creates comfortable and sufficient daylight with which to meet the functional requirements of the space and improves access to views. In typical open offices that have areas farther than thirty feet from a window, the contrast from the window wall is so intense that blinds are required nearly all of the time in order to maintain comfort. Because contrast between the perimeter window wall and the other surfaces in the space, including the back wall, is kept to a manageable level, occupants are able to enjoy views that would otherwise be uncomfortable to look at or concealed by blinds.

Design for the mutually reinforcing provision of both daylight and view continues in the space planning and interior design and layout of the offices. Shared open office environments tend to be occupied nearly continuously during the workday, yet single private offices are often unoccupied more than half of the time during regular office hours. For this reason, private offices were located at the interior wall, away from the perimeter, yet adjacent to the overhead skylights, ensuring an equitable distribution of light and views. Curtis elaborates: "We wanted to figure out the 'magic dimension' for the open offices, keeping them shallow and burying the individual offices in the back, which was a little bit risky; if you put them out there [at the perimeter], it blows the whole concept."

The commitment to daylight and view is carried into the furniture design as well. Office partitions are kept low and unobtrusive at forty-two inches in height, parallel to the perimeter windows. This allows daylight to be distributed from the side and provides open-view corridors across the building section. Taller partitions are perpendicular to the glazing and rise to sixty-five inches, which affords privacy and allows for storage without compromising the views or creating dark shadows.

PUBLIC AREAS

Transparency and openness in government were the metaphorical drivers for the civic presence and visual character of the building. Designers enlisted daylight as a primary design element on behalf of this goal. Many of the public areas use an architectural language of prominent wall surfaces that are washed with skylight provided by glass reveals where a wall meets the ceiling. This lends a dynamic and dramatic quality to the public lobbies and circulation ways. Washing the primary vertical surfaces with daylight has the effect of bringing out objects within the building that have levels of brightness comparable to the intensity of outdoor luminosity. This creates a remarkable sense of transparency between the building interior and the approach from outside. From within, expanses of glass offer occupants a continuous orientation to the landmarks that define Port Orchard: Puget Sound and the Olympic Mountains. These relationships coupled with the steep slope of the site aid in way-finding and provide spaces for gathering, relaxing, and meditating in places that capture the essence of landscape and light in Kitsap County.

AWARDS

» Sustainable Buildings Industry Council (SBIC) Beyond Green Award, 2009
» Honor Award, AIA Northwest and Pacific Region, 2008
» Merit Award, AIA Seattle Chapter, 2008
» Merit Award, AIA Washington Civic Design Awards, 2007

7

"Daylighting was a primary factor in the layout of the building from the start."
—Doug Cooper, McKibben + Cooper Architects

MCKIBBEN + COOPER ARCHITECTS. PROJECT LOCATION: GARDEN CITY, IDAHO

Lolly Wyatt Center
Head Start and Early Head Start

Exterior, looking north. Photo: C. Meek and K. Van Den Wymelenberg.

Interior, looking northwest from within piazza. Photo: C. Meek and K. Van Den Wymelenberg.

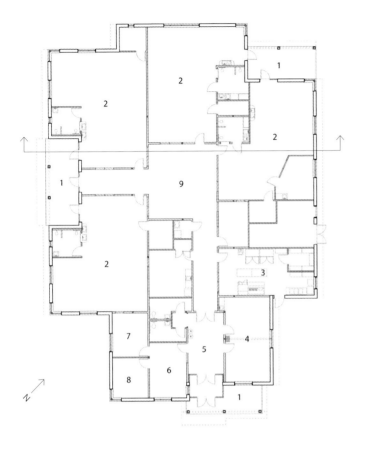

Lolly Wyatt Center, Head Start
and Early Head Start Center
1 Porch
2 Classroom
3 Kitchen
4 Conference Room
5 Entry
6 Reception
7 Meeting
8 Office
9 Piazza

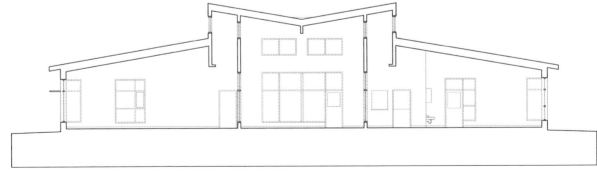

Interior, looking south in the south classroom.
Photo: C. Meek and K. Van Den Wymelenberg.

THE LOLLY WYATT CENTER, HEAD START AND EARLY HEAD START, AIMS TO knit together the diversity of the surrounding community while creating a safe and productive learning atmosphere for the children in the Head Start programs. The building is designed in accordance with the principles of Reggio Emilia, which promote community engagement in the education of young children. The design challenge was to create an open and engaging place for learning that was connected to the community.

The building is home to an early childhood education group and is situated in the middle of a transitioning community. Historically a light-industrial zone, the area is now evolving toward a mixed-use commercial and residential zone. The Head Start program was part of the impetus for these changes, and the community engagement promoted by the Reggio Emilia educational philosophy was an important aspect of the neighborhood's revitalization. These factors also had an impact on the development of the daylighting strategy.

BUILT ENVIRONMENT AND LEARNING

In keeping with the Reggio Emilia approach, the community is welcomed into the building specifically through the use of the piazza as a gathering space. Also integral to the Reggio Emilia approach is a high-quality physical environment with ample daylight, transparent interior partitions, and windows designed with the size and perspective of the children in mind.

BUILDING ORGANIZATION

McKibben + Cooper Architects would have preferred to organize all classrooms with a southern exposure, which would support daylighting goals, but the site constraints did not allow this approach. Instead, the classroom spaces were organized around a central piazza, a flexible-use space, much like the layout of an Italian village. For this reason, each classroom

needed to be designed individually in response to the specific daylight characteristics resulting from the multiple window orientations. Perimeter windows were intended to provide functional daylight only to the activity spaces near the edge of the classrooms, while large clerestory windows, the primary source of illumination for each classroom, enliven the interior walls with daylight.

PUTTING THE DAYLIGHT WHERE IT IS NEEDED

Although the piazza is a community gathering space and major building organizational element, it is not daylit at the expense of the classrooms. As is the case with most schools, the classrooms at this Head Start are the most commonly occupied spaces, require the highest levels of illumination,

Interior, looking northeast in the south classroom. Photo: C. Meek and K. Van Den Wymelenberg.

Interior, looking northwest in the west classroom. Photo: C. Meek and K. Van Den Wymelenberg.

Interior, looking east in the west classroom. Photo: C. Meek and K. Van Den Wymelenberg.

and demand the most stringent standards of visual comfort. Therefore they received the most daylight design attention. According to Doug Cooper of McKibben + Cooper Architects, lead designer for the Head Start spaces, "A primary goal was to light each classroom with as much indirect natural light as possible to reduce the reliance on electric light. This was especially important since the classrooms were so large [1,200 square feet], and light from the [perimeter] windows did not reach in very far."

While each classroom receives functional daylight from at least two and often three edges of the room, the most significant daylighting design element is the band of clerestory windows facilitated by a butterfly roof high above the piazza. The roof extends to an enclosure wall about six feet past the interior-most wall of each classroom. The clerestories underneath the butterfly roof allow daylight to illuminate the interior surfaces of the classrooms directly. Secondarily, the daylight is redirected into the piazza through large relight windows adjacent to the exterior clerestories as well as through lower view windows between the classroom and the piazza. Cooper notes, "The configuration of the plan almost dictated that we use the same device to both light the rear of the classrooms through indirect light and pass light through the clerestories to light the piazza." This is a refreshing departure from common practice. Far too often, the primary daylight design element is focused on circulation ways, resulting in over-illuminated hallways where lighting requirements are minimal. Then designers attempt to borrow this daylight for the primarily occupied spaces, such as classrooms, where lighting requirements are higher. This approach rarely provides functional daylight illumination to the most crucial spaces where people spend the most time and can detract from visual comfort in both space types. Conversely, at the Head Start, the solution was to first daylight the spaces where people spend the most time and then share the light with adjacent spaces.

VIEWS, SHADING, AND USERS

The exterior walls are composed of Durisol blocks, a baked fibrous product about the size of conventional concrete masonry units. This construction methodology creates deep windowsills and the feeling of a substantial and massive structure. The deep window reveals reduce the expanse of the view to the exterior, providing directed views while still giving the impression of transparency from the outside. The deep reveals also supply some solar shading.

Somewhat counter to the daylighting goals, the children's toilet rooms are located within the classrooms at the perimeter of the building due to programmatic priorities. This decision had two significant results. First, the toilet rooms somewhat limit the penetration of daylight from the perimeter and contribute to the need for supplemental daylight at the in-board wall. Second, the perimeter location blocks some undesirable exterior views while also directing visual attention to the central community gathering space.

In addition to the deep window reveals, simple, exterior, perforated metal overhangs bounce some light through the upper portion of the glass while shading the view window during the hottest months of the year. An interesting aspect of the project is that it uses no interior fabric or louver blinds. In a few locations, users have modified their spaces with various types of shading elements; however, for the most part, the windows remain free of any interior shading and continue to offer access to daylight. This is possible due to the deep windowsills, fixed external shading, and mature landscaping that work in synergy to minimize direct glare from sun penetration. While these are important steps toward reducing glare, by themselves, they would not have been sufficient. Two other factors contribute to the success of this design solution. First, the flexibility of use patterns afforded by early childhood education increases user tolerance of short periods of direct sun. Second, the daylight provided by clerestories at

Exterior of southeast elevation. Photo:
C. Meek and K. Van Den Wymelenberg.

the back wall dramatically reduces contrast and balances spatial luminosity, which improves visual comfort within the space on both sunny and cloudy days. The significant amount of daylight introduced to classroom spaces where people spend the most time allows Head Start to function for substantial periods without the use of electric lighting. Some teachers perceive this to be more calming to students, and it also saves energy.

"The biggest challenge was to understand the dynamics between creating access to daylight and ventilation because 80 percent of this building is naturally ventilated."
—Anne Schopf, AIA Design Partner, Mahlum

MAHLUM, OLYMPIA. PROJECT LOCATION: WASHINGTON

The Evergreen State College Seminar 2 Building

Exterior courtyard between academic clusters, looking north. Photo: C. Meek and C. Von Rueden.

Top-floor art studios with clerestory monitors. Photo: C. Meek and C. Von Rueden.

Level 1

Level 2 & 3

Level 4

The Evergreen State College:
Seminar 2 Building
1 Entry
2 Break-Out Room
3 Lecture Hall
4 Workshop
5 Offices
6 Homeroom
7 Seminar Room
8 Class Lab
9 Eco-Roof

N

THE EVERGREEN STATE COLLEGE IS A SMALL LIBERAL ARTS COLLEGE THAT was founded in 1971 just outside of Olympia. The campus sits within a 1,000-acre forested enclosure apart from the city center to the east. When campus planners decided to build a major new facility, they evaluated a number of locations before selecting an infill site between two existing campus buildings and the central plaza. This was intended to increase density in the central campus. Concerns about reducing forest cover in part shaped the layout of the five semiautonomous academic clusters that compose the 150,000-square-foot complex. Each cluster includes faculty offices, art studios, classrooms, and informal study areas. The college has a tradition of progressive leadership with respect to environmental advocacy and social responsibility. As part of Mahlum's extensive pre-design process, an early survey asked the entire faculty which office they would prefer: one with operable windows, no air-conditioning, and high ceilings, or a more conventional office with air-conditioning and no operable windows. The answers nearly unanimously favored operable windows.

BUILDING SECTION GEOMETRY

The geometric organization of the building arises from ideas about periods of occupancy and user comfort relative to light, heat, and air. The organization reflects a hierarchy of use patterns, specific durations of occupancy, requirements for visual acuity, spatial needs, and the expected hours and months of use relative to outdoor weather conditions. This prioritization

Entry lobby looking south, with views to courtyard landscape. Photo: C. Meek and C. Von Rueden.

Interior corridor light and ventilation well. Photo: C. Meek and C. Von Rueden.

Courtyard between academic clusters with exterior solar shades. Photo: C. Meek and C. Von Rueden.

manifests itself in the fundamental building planning. Discussions with building users revealed that most faculty were in their offices during the morning and midday rather than during evening hours. This led the design team to locate these offices to the west side of the building, where limited occupancy and low occupant density would minimize the negative effects of late afternoon overheating and glare from low-angle direct sunlight.

Classrooms and larger lecture halls were located to the east so that they would not become overheated during the hottest hours of the afternoon. This might have posed challenges to visual comfort for early morning classes; however, limited glazing and a tall stand of mature conifers offer protection against glare. Large trees reduce daylight levels in many of the classrooms. The designers considered this an acceptable trade-off for two reasons. First, these spaces are used intermittently, and occupants rarely spend more than two hours continuously in any of the classrooms or seminar rooms. Second, the increased use of audiovisual technology allowed for lower ambient light levels. Art studios were prioritized on the upper floor in order to take advantage of the most optimum source of daylight on this site, directly overhead. To allow for daylight and air in the space between the faculty offices and the classrooms, a three-story interior light well cuts between these two primary building zones, creating the opportunity for informal study areas. This configuration permits daylight access throughout the facility while prioritizing the amount and character of light relative to the visual tasks and times of use. Anne Schopf, partner at Mahlum and design team leader, says of the project's key features: "In this facility of over 150,000 square feet, more than five distinct buildings, there is no space that does not have access to views and daylight." She adds, "If the power goes out, there is really no excuse for anyone to go home."

Informal study alcove looking southwest, with exterior shading and interior light shelf.
Photo: C. Meek and C. Von Rueden.

ART STUDIOS

Since each building cluster is directly adjacent to old-growth conifers, the greatest source of daylight is from above. The architects took advantage of this by locating the visual arts studios on the top floor of each building. Lower floors, not directly under a roof, must rely on daylight from the side via vertical windows. In an art studio, however, users need vertical wall space for displaying work and prize opaque wall over windows. Therefore, bringing in diffuse daylight from above is an ideal approach. The design team at Mahlum created a daylighting model, which it used to test a range of design options.

The goals were to illuminate the horizontal surfaces evenly across the large art studio volume while blocking all direct sunlight and providing a pleasant distribution of light. The final design configuration takes the form of a series of skylight monitors organized in concert with the large beams that carry the weight of the roof and allow for a large, unobstructed studio space. Skylight apertures are positioned asymmetrically on each side of

Above:

Top-floor art studio looking south. Daylight from above allows for use of extensive interior wall area for artwork and display. Photo: C. Meek and C. Von Rueden.

Clerestory monitor in art studios, with north- and south-facing clerestories. Photo: C. Meek and C. Von Rueden.

Opposite:

Clerestory monitor in art studios, with north- and south-facing clerestories. Structural steel beams serve as direct sunlight control. Photo: C. Meek and C. Von Rueden.

Top-floor interior corridor light and ventilation well. Photo: C. Meek and C. Von Rueden.

the deep wide-flange steel beams that carry the roof. The beams were designed, in part, to serve as a shading element and to redirect direct sunlight. The monitors admit direct sunlight from the southern sky, but the geometric relationship between the steel beams and the south-facing glass prevents sun from entering the central studio floor. This ensures that even the steepest direct summertime sunlight does not enter the studio or cause glare. The north side of the monitor is pulled farther away from the structural beam, allowing for abundant diffuse illumination from the overcast and the dark blue northern sky on clear days. A secondary east-facing clerestory balances the brightness of the vertical surfaces across the building section and allows direct morning sunlight to animate the wall surface adjacent to the sculpture studios. Sheer curtains diffuse this direct sunlight when required. The stark white palette of the interior finishes enhances the inter-reflection of daylight within the space and reveals the subtle differences in chromacity and intensity of each source of daylight.

SEMINAR ROOMS AND CLASSROOMS

The architects designed seminar rooms and classrooms so that they foster a close link to the adjacent outdoor environment, giving a sense of connection to the campus and reinforcing a well-known preference for views to nature. The views from classrooms and the larger seminar rooms are predominantly to the east. This is commonly a difficult challenge due to glare during morning classes; however, the combination of very tall, painstakingly preserved conifers located just feet from the east-facing windows and exterior vertical-fin shading devices angled toward the north substantially reduces the glare from direct sunlight. Some classrooms are illuminated with daylight from two sides, ensuring that when one window poses a threat to visual comfort because of low sun angles, there is a strong likelihood that the other will not. Since classrooms are occupied for short periods of time, as opposed to the long periods of occupancy in the art stu-

Classroom with daylight from two sides
and shallow section depth. Photo: C. Meek
and C. Von Rueden.

Exterior of academic cluster, looking northeast.
Photo: C. Meek and C. Von Rueden.

Channel glass stairwell with operable windows.
Photo: C. Meek and C. Von Rueden.

dios, daylight distribution from one side, where unavoidable, was deemed acceptable. In practice, this is a good fit with the relatively flexible visual comfort demands of interactive discussion groups or slide lectures, the dominant use for these spaces. Daylight becomes a fundamental aspect of the classroom locations and organization and at the same time offers a remarkable connection to the surrounding forested campus.

FACULTY OFFICES AND CIRCULATION WAYS

A key component of the building design is that it enables natural ventilation and supplies daylight to the center of the structure. A large overhead skylight washes the cast-in-place concrete wall surface with daylight, bringing drama and visibility to an otherwise dark interior space. The presence of daylight here is the by-product of the decision to allow sunlight to heat the mass of the corridor walls in order to drive the stack effect, a means of natural ventilation, which draws warm air from the adjacent classrooms, offices, and seminar rooms. The result is a visual experience composed of a rich, dynamic distribution of light along with exceptionally high indoor air quality. Faculty offices are located to the west of the circulation way. Shallow office depths and bright surface finishes in the upper zone of these spaces allow for adequate daylight distribution from modest apertures on the perimeter of the building, while horizontal exterior sunshades extend the cool and glare-free period in the offices by several hours during the warmest, sunniest times of the year.

INFORMAL STUDY AREAS

Study alcoves engage the edges of the circulation way between the classrooms and the faculty offices. These informal gathering spaces find their form in the spaces between the primary program elements. Some face south, some west, and some north. They are by nature idiosyncratic. Some have solar shading, and others offer unimpeded views to the campus and adjoining gardens. The eclectic character of the daylight gives these spaces a playful drama. Site visits indicate that they are in almost constant use. Students are free to sit where they prefer and can choose a location and spatial orientation that suits their immediate needs. These conditions would not perform well in a scenario in which students' desks were fixed in place. In this case, however, occupants are able to organize their activities around the prevailing patterns of daylight, rather than daylight distribution being designed around specific human activities.

AWARDS

» AIA Committee on Architecture for Education (CAE), Award of Excellence, 2007
» USGBC Living Building Challenge, Demonstrated Leadership in Indoor Quality, 2007
» AIA Northwest and Pacific Region, Honor Award, 2006
» AIA Seattle Honor Awards, 2006
» Council of Educational Facility Planners International (CEFPI) International Project of Distinction Award, 2006
» Edwin F. Guth Interior Lighting Design Award, IESNA, Puget Sound Section, 2006
» Energy and Environmental Design Award, Illuminating Engineering Society of North America (IESNA), Puget Sound Section, 2006
» AIA COTE Top Ten Green Projects, 2005
» AIA Washington Council Civic Design, Honor Award, 2005
» USGBC, LEED Gold, 2005

"The Shoreline Recycling and Transfer Station is rapidly becoming the benchmark for sustainable facility design of this type."

—American Public Works Association

KPG ARCHITECTS AND ENGINEERS. PROJECT LOCATION: SHORELINE, WASHINGTON

Shoreline Recycling and Transfer Station

Exterior view looking northwest.
Photo: C. Meek.

Self-haul tipping wall and metal recycling.
Photo: C. Meek.

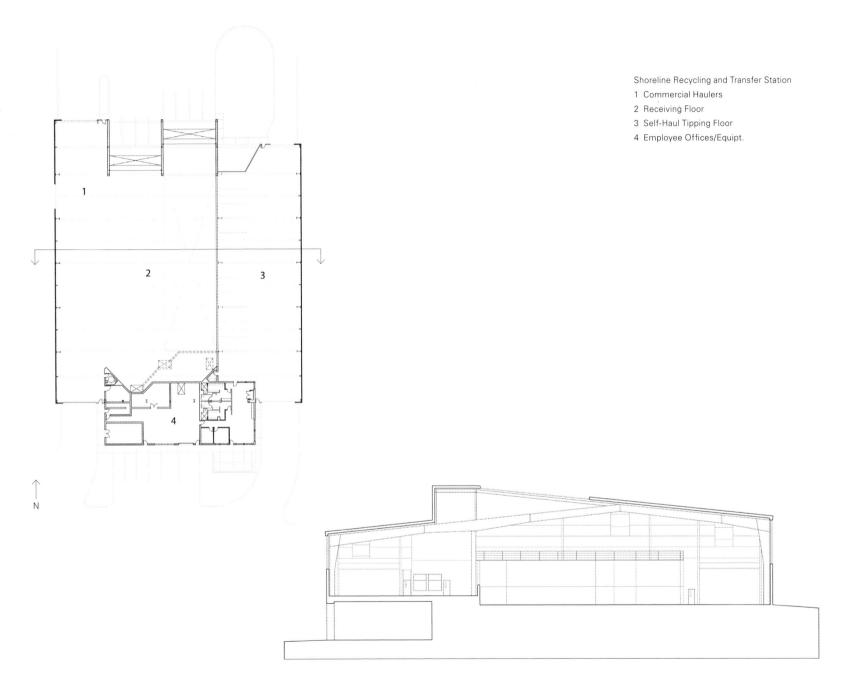

Shoreline Recycling and Transfer Station
1 Commercial Haulers
2 Receiving Floor
3 Self-Haul Tipping Floor
4 Employee Offices/Equipt.

N

THE SHORELINE RECYCLING AND TRANSFER STATION IS A 76,000-SQUARE-foot facility designed to provide a location for the collection and sorting of recyclables, yard waste, and solid waste. When King County, Washington, embarked on the creation of a new facility, it decided to completely rethink the notion of "the dump." This included a reassessment of everything from storm water collection, noise, landscape, ecology, and energy use. "The design team was afforded a full opportunity to pursue the range of solutions to achieve synergies, which are essential to attain the highest LEED project certification levels," explains Doug Brinley, principal architect at KPG and lead designer for the facility. Improving the quality of the interior environment for all workers was a particular focus of the design effort.

Historically, urban transfer stations have been dark, cavernous enclosures illuminated by bleak high-pressure sodium lights with only a meager daylight contribution, usually from light that might sneak in through an open garage door. The Shoreline Recycling and Transfer Station completely upends the paradigm of waste management facilities, creating a new model for contemporary, high-bay, daylit industrial space.

PROCESS

This project poses a unique contrast to many other daylit spaces, first, in its expansive scale and, second, in being an almost exclusively unconditioned space. The facility incorporates natural ventilation but has no mechanical heating or cooling within the high-bay volumes or at the self-haul tipping wall, where users dispose of unwanted material.

Commercial hauler floor, from mezzanine.
Photo: C. Meek.

View to tipping floor, from operations room.
Photo: C. Meek.

A central diffusing skylight illuminates the interior of the transfer station. Photo: C. Meek.

One of the primary concerns in designing any building for both daylighting and energy efficiency is the relationship between aperture area and insulated opaque envelope. Since this building is not mechanically heated or cooled, the aperture area was not a limiting factor, and decisions on the size and location of glazing were based largely on sufficient daylight distribution. For this reason, the design team was able to be far more aggressive with daylighting performance goals than would have otherwise been feasible. The team chose a cellular polycarbonate material as the primary glazing material due to its weather-tightness, spanning capability, and relatively high visible-light transmission. A massive skylight centered over the receiving floor and tipping wall provides diffuse daylight at illumination levels close to those found outdoors. This strategy provides sufficient horizontal illumination for tasks; however, creating a high-quality visual environment required additional apertures in order to produce a balanced composition of light. At the east- and west-facing walls, the entire wall section above fifteen feet is glazed with the same translucent polycarbonate as used in the roof, which provides illumination at the perimeter and brightness across the entire building section. This is critical to successful daylighting in almost any space, but even more so in such a large volume. The perimeter clerestory directs daylight onto the otherwise dark, opaque ceiling surface directly adjacent to the large central skylight, thus minimizing contrast and improving visual comfort. Since the indoor daylight illumination is at such high levels and because the transfer station's operating hours are closely linked with the hours of daylight, the requirement for supplementary electric lighting is minimal year-round.

Besides saving energy, the daylighting strategy also contributes to a safer work environment. Vehicular navigation is one of the primary activities that take place within transfer stations. Motorists and truck operators drive from the bright outdoors into a typically darker enclosed space. The human eye adapts to a wide range of light levels, but the transition occurs slowly, and more slowly when going from bright to dim. Histori-

Interior, looking north, with translucent clerestories at east and west walls illuminating perimeter drive aisles. Photo: C. Meek.

Art installation by Carol dePelecyn at entry
and exit drives. Photo: C. Meek.

cally, non-daylit transfer station designs have neglected this phenomenon, and users go almost instantaneously from outdoor illumination levels of 5,000 foot-candles or greater to interior conditions of less than 20 foot-candles of electric illumination, which results in decreased visibility during a critical period as they navigate around other vehicles and station staff. Relying on daylight as the primary source of interior illumination sharply reduces this concern. High levels of interior daylight illumination soften the otherwise abrupt transition from the bright daylit outdoors to the interior space. Furthermore, the dynamic nature of daylight meshes well with this design strategy. As outdoor illumination levels decrease at the end of a day or during times of heavy cloud cover, the amount of light at the interior decreases proportionally.

The Shoreline transfer station provides daylight in a manner that is resilient, functional, and, perhaps most important, appropriately tuned to its users' expectations and visual systems based on time of day and outdoor light conditions. The facility provides a safe, high-quality visual environment, with the added benefit of delivering substantial reductions in lighting energy use, an apt metaphor for an institution whose primary mission is reducing waste.

AWARDS

» American Council of Engineering Companies (ACEC), Gold
Engineering Excellence Award in the Environmental category, 2009

» ACEC, Judges' Award for Sustainable Design, 2009

» ACEC, National Finalist, 2009

» American Public Works Association (APWA), National Project
of the Year for the Environment, $5–25 million category, 2009

» APWA Washington State Chapter, Project of the Year for
the Environment, $5–25 million category, 2009

» Northwest Construction Consumer Council (NWCCC),
2008 Green Project of the Year, 2009

» AIA, Honorable Mention for "What Makes It Green?" 2008

» Northwest Construction Consumer Council (NWCCC),
Grand Project of the Year, 2008

» Solid Waste Association of North America (SWANA),
National Innovation Award, 2008

» USGBC, LEED Platinum, 2008 (the first industrial project
in the world to receive the LEED Platinum certification)

» King County, Excellence in Building Green, 2007

» Thornton Creek Alliance, certificate, 2004

10

"Our contribution is to show strategies that provide a garden for ourselves as well as passers-by. We beckon, but we also resist."
—Dwaine Carver, Trout Architects

TROUT ARCHITECTS. PROJECT LOCATION: BOISE, IDAHO

Jacqueline Crist Gallery

Exterior, looking southwest. Photo:
C. Meek and K. Van Den Wymelenberg.

Interior, looking east in gallery. Photo:
C. Meek and K. Van Den Wymelenberg.

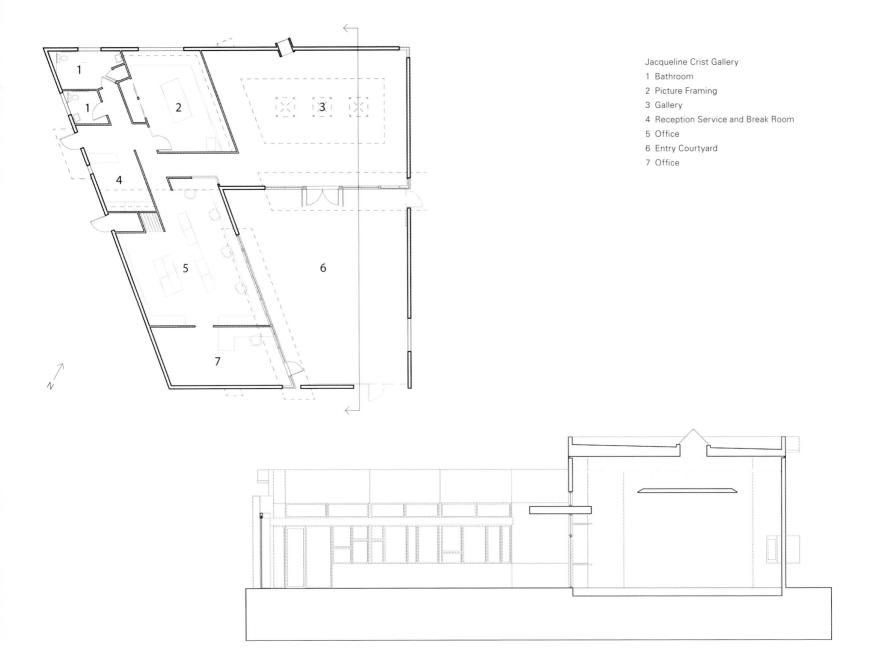

Jacqueline Crist Gallery

1 Bathroom
2 Picture Framing
3 Gallery
4 Reception Service and Break Room
5 Office
6 Entry Courtyard
7 Office

THE JACQUELINE CRIST GALLERY, FOUNDED BY IDAHO NATIVE JACQUELINE Crist in 1995, opened its doors in 2005. The gallery represents artists from Idaho and the Pacific Northwest and curates artist-specific and thematic shows in all types of media. The building is located in a light-industrial area at the western edge of downtown Boise, on a former brownfield, hemmed in by a mixture of low-rise buildings, commercial services, surface parking lots, and a tangle of four-lane arterial roadways. The site is an irregularly shaped trapezoid with a sliver of land to the south that grows wider toward the north. According to designer Dwaine Carver, the banal surroundings of the site were simply a reality. "Our contribution is to show strategies that provide a garden for ourselves as well as passers-by. We beckon, but we also resist. For example, the corner windows and the 'box' window aestheticize traffic as well as the mountain front views. A courtyard wall bisects a garden, leaving a portion for the public. We participate, but in doing so, we also make a realm for ourselves." The gallery turns inward, creating a layer of separation from the chaotic context while at the same time being careful not to extricate itself from the neighborhood. It serves as respite but selectively receives and reflects the varied context. Carver says, "It is its own place, simultaneously engaging and shutting out the site."

COURTYARD AND GALLERY

The building is constructed with a minimalist and mostly opaque hard-coat stucco skin. Its form is a stressed L shape, and fifteen-foot-tall outdoor walls complete a rectilinear form and enclose a sizable open-air courtyard. Carver notes that the decision to create a "southeast-facing courtyard drove the site plan and the form of the building. Volumes were established and then perforated. This was an operation driven simultaneously by day-lighting strategies, views, and geometry." Small sliced openings in the courtyard walls afford glimpses to and from the neighborhood. Oversize

View toward exterior context. Photo:
C. Meek and K. Van Den Wymelenberg.

Interior gallery window detail. Photo:
C. Meek and K. Van Den Wymelenberg.

Exterior, looking northwest into courtyard.
Photo: C. Meek and K. Van Den Wymelenberg.

Exterior, looking southeast into courtyard.
Photo: C. Meek and K. Van Den Wymelenberg.

Interior, looking west in gallery. Photo:
C. Meek and K. Van Den Wymelenberg.

Interior, looking east in gallery. Photo:
C. Meek and K. Van Den Wymelenberg.

sliding doors and smaller standard doors allow physical access and more or less visual connection to the surrounding neighborhood as desired. While the gallery proper is the primary enclosed space, the open-air courtyard mediates the interaction between the building and the neighborhood.

The outdoor courtyard is used as an extension of the gallery and an event space for openings and exhibitions. The courtyard and the gallery space are separated by a glazed curtain-wall system that can be completely retracted by opening six large swinging glass doors to create one large indoor-outdoor space. The gallery floor and ceiling are made of exposed oriented strand board, and open-web metal ceiling joists are revealed throughout the building. Stark white walls are articulated with a one-inch reveal above the floor and at the ceiling, providing subtle shadows and a visual separation that complement the change in materials.

The gallery was designed to function under daylight conditions. Carver states that he wanted to "quietly implicate the building into the art; a black-

box approach is much more limited in its participation with art if the light is only artificial and static."

The high demand for wall space as a display surface for artwork dictated that there would be relatively few openings in vertical surfaces. The limited openings in the vertical planes are quite small and are intended primarily to frame views to specific neighborhood icons and the mountains beyond downtown to the northeast. The corners of the gallery were subtracted and provide a modest amount of daylight on the adjacent walls but are not an effective daylight strategy by themselves. Without supplemental daylight, there would not be enough brightness on the interior surfaces of the gallery and on the artwork to compete with the brightness of the views to the surrounding streetscape. Therefore, these narrow openings are supplemented with three simple pyramidal skylights and a wall of glazing to the southeast that forms the threshold with the courtyard. The skylights are inexpensive, clear plastic pyramids and are tucked behind a large opaque

"cloud" structure mounted about five feet below the ceiling. The cloud element is composed of a wooden frame with drywall and plaster articulated with a knife edge to reduce its visual weight within the space. This element serves three primary purposes. First, it blocks direct sunlight from penetrating the gallery through the clear skylights. Second, it redirects light onto the adjacent walls and ceiling of the gallery. Third, it eliminates the line of sight to the skylights for gallery patrons and produces a minimal aesthetic.

SOLAR SHADING

Preservation of the artworks displayed made keeping direct sunlight to a minimum a priority. However, completely eliminating direct sun penetration in the gallery would have been detrimental to the overall success of the space. According to Carver, "Allowing sunlight to directly strike the north interior wall of the gallery a few weeks each year was a concession to the

Interior, looking southeast in gallery. Photo:
C. Meek and K. Van Den Wymelenberg.

extraordinary and unacceptable measures we would have had to take otherwise. We felt the payback was a space with living light." The goal was to design an autonomous system that solved most of the direct sun problem. The solution was to employ several layers of protection that work to eliminate and soften the sun penetration. Outdoor courtyard walls eliminate low-angle and off-axis sun that would otherwise enter from the southeast curtain-wall and shine into the gallery. The cloud element eliminates almost all of the direct sun from the clear skylights and restricts sun penetration to the highest part of the north gallery wall. Vegetation in the courtyard filters high-angle sunlight that enters the gallery, and a soffit just above the glass curtain-wall acts as a shading device. Finally, sheer curtains can be drawn to reduce the intensity of light from the adjacent sun-filled courtyard.

AWARDS

» Boise Mayor's Excellence in Design Awards, 2008
» AIA Idaho Chapter, Award of Honor in Architecture, 2006

11

"The rhythm and geometries of the agricultural landscape, along with the craft, technology, and patterns of wine production, shape the architecture and landscape of the winery."

—Mike Januik, winemaker

MITHUN. PROJECT LOCATION: WOODINVILLE, WASHINGTON

Novelty Hill–Januik Winery

Exterior view looking north at bocce court.
Photo: C. Meek and M. Foley.

An overhead skylight illuminates café tables, while transparent skylights wash artwork and concrete walls with light. Photo: C. Meek and M. Foley.

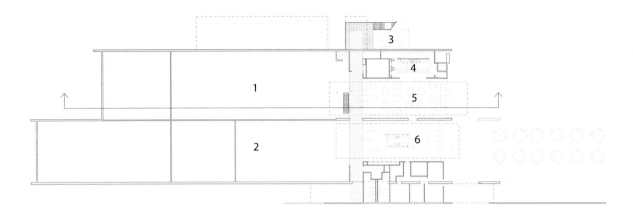

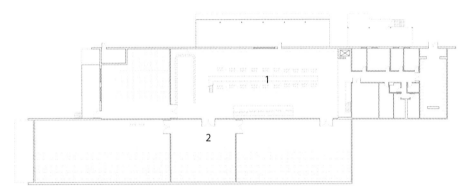

N

Novelty Hill–Januik Winery

1 Upper Floor Plan
2 Tank and Bottling (Below)
3 Barrel Room (Below)
4 Meeting Room
5 Kitchen
6 Banquet Room
7 Tasting Room
8 Lower Floor Plan
9 Tank and Bottling
10 Barrel Room

Tasting room, looking east with transparent skylights washing tilt-up concrete walls.
Photo: C. Meek and M. Foley.

THE NOVELTY HILL–JANUIK WINERY SERVES AS THE TASTING ROOM AND PRO-duction facility for two independent wineries, Novelty Hill Wines and Januik Winery. Designed by Mithun, a Seattle-based architecture, planning, and interior design firm, and landscape architect Katherine Anderson, the winery provides a dramatic, contemporary setting for wine tasting, production, bottling, and cask aging, as well as fine dining, weddings, and corporate events. The grounds offer winemaker Mike Januik a place in which to exer-cise his craft. In describing the facility, the owner notes that "the rhythm and geometries of the agricultural landscape, along with the craft, technol-ogy and patterns of wine production, shape the architecture and landscape of the winery, drawing on both the linear rows of grapes in a vineyard and the rows of tanks in a winery—that guides everything from the shape of the parking lot to the footprint of the building and sets up a rhythm of paral-lel shifting walls."[2]

Mithun's projects provide leadership in sustainable design, and the Novelty Hill–Januik Winery is no exception. At the outset, the designers engaged the Seattle Daylighting Lab and the University of Oregon's Energy Studies in Buildings Laboratory led by Professor G. Z. Brown for early design guidance with respect to climate response, daylighting, and spatial program patterns of energy use. One aspect of this collaboration was daylighting programming, which consists of assessing the quality, intensity, visual comfort requirements, and experiential goals of daylight relative to each spatial program element. Then, patterns of use, occupancy hours, and geometric requirements are considered along with suitable orientation and potential aperture strategies for meeting performance criteria. Daylighting programming makes the architectural implications of achieving effective daylight and views among the central components of the building organization, and it establishes appropriate spatial relationships between functional program requirements and daylight and energy performance.

Transparent skylights wash the space concrete walls in the tasting room, while electrically illuminated pendants provide visual focus and task illumination at the bar. Photo: C. Meek and M. Foley.

Exterior view looking south to terraced gardens. Photo: C. Meek and M. Foley.

Banquet seating illuminated with daylight. Photo: C. Meek and M. Foley.

This approach recognizes that each space type has specific daylighting needs and goals and that what might be a perfectly acceptable experience of daylight and sunlight in one space might be entirely inappropriate in another. Designers not only can tune the daylighting design to the specific program elements or space type but allow for a dynamic range of luminous experiences as users move through the building. The quality of light evolves deliberately from space to space. For example, the tasting room is a dramatic and informal setting with minimal control over daylight, while the tank and bottling areas require a bright and even distribution of diffuse light for their industrial activities. By contrast, the barrel room offers the cool dark enclosure one would expect to find in a cave for the aging and storage of wine. Each of these experiences is shaped by specific and distinct approaches to the luminous environment.

TASTING ROOM AND CAFÉ

The winery is loosely divided into a public retail and hospitality zone and a series of more private, industrial, "back of house" spaces that compose the winemaking studios and barrel room. These elements are broken up by a series of linear concrete walls that functionally separate the spaces but have glass partitions that visually connect the tasting and banquet rooms to the winemaking process and equipment.

The tasting room and café provide a dynamic setting and welcome for visitors to the winery. Since the visual tasks here are not demanding—sipping wine, chatting with the servers, selecting bottles—the daylighting requirements are flexible, allowing for patches of direct sunlight, brightness, and darkness that add drama and a hint of mystery to the space. Daylight sources surround and enliven the restrained palette of construction materials that make up the volume. Vertical glazing to the south allows for views to the terraced gardens and bocce courts, borrowing from the luminous surfaces of decomposed granite that makes up much of the surrounding ground plane, while a deep glass canopy and an allée of deciduous ash trees temper the southern sun. A large skylight provides horizontal illumination to the café tables at the north end of the space. The primary vertical surfaces span the length of the space and are positioned adjacent to transparent skylights that allow a play of direct-beam and diffuse sky illumination that depicts the passing of time and weather on the shifting planes of concrete that make up the winery's walls. At the wine-tasting bar, a glowing array of custom, electrically illuminated pendant fixtures provides a consistent visual focal point while lighting the countertop and bringing out the color and clarity of the wines. In this arrangement, the central tasting bar anchors the space by meeting the more predictable space lighting needs. The surfaces surrounding it shift from dark to light, sun-raked to glowing, with diffuse oyster-hued skylight marking the passage of time and the seasons that produce the world-class wines of Washington State.

The banquet room and kitchen employ similar goals and strategies, though the primary visual focus is the culinary activity of the chefs who work in a partially open kitchen. The tables are illuminated with candlelight, while either daylight or darkness claims the vertical surfaces and views to the terraces beyond. Since the banquet room is occasionally used for audiovisual presentations, motorized louvers in the skylight wells allow for room darkening when required.

BARREL ROOM

For proper aging, wine must be kept at a near-constant fifty-five to sixty degrees Fahrenheit. For this reason, the barrel room was located at the west edge of the site, where the slope of the grade allows it to be largely subterranean, using the constant cool temperature of the earth in the Puget Sound region to its advantage. The barrel room is rarely occupied and has very limited visual task requirements, so the role of daylight is limited. In order to avoid unnecessary thermal loads and improve energy

Tank and bottling room diffusely illuminated at high levels with skylights. Photo: C. Meek and M. Foley.

Barrel room, with minimal light levels. Photo: C. Meek and M. Foley.

efficiency, daylight apertures were restricted to a few very specific locations. Since views to the barrel room from the café and tasting room are an important part of the visual experience of the winery, one skylight was placed at the far end of the barrel room, allowing visitors to perceive the depth of the concrete enclosure. A second skylight was placed where it would illuminate the texture of the face of the barrels. This strengthens the perceptual experience in two key ways. The barrels become glowing objects in an otherwise dark space, and the wash of light on the back wall of the barrel room enables visual transparency through the glass that separates the cool barrel room from the much warmer tasting area and café. Without the skylights, the glass would not appear transparent because the brightness of the daylit café would be reflected in the window of the substantially darker barrel room. This strategy allows for energy efficiency while heightening the visual experience of this crucial component of the winemaking process.

TANK AND BOTTLING AREA

The tank and bottling facility is occupied nearly all day, and the activities that take place in this part of the winery are among the most visually demanding. Both the architectural character and the daylighting design reflect these requirements. Reading sensitive gauges, operating bottling equipment, taking notes, and using visual display terminals all demand a high level of visual acuity. The intention of the daylighting design was to provide effective illumination to meet those needs while taking care not to create opportunities for glare or excessive visual contrast. Skylights were carefully located in both plan and section where they would ensure shadow-free illumination between the massive stainless steel tanks. The use of translucent light-diffusing skylights ensures that direct sunlight never interferes with visual comfort by providing a constant, highly uniform distribution of light regardless of sky conditions. The interior surfaces were painted white or left as unfinished concrete, which increases interior reflectivity and reduces contrast between adjacent vertical planes in the occupants' field of view.

Appropriate daylighting criteria vary as widely as the activities that buildings are designed to support. A successful daylighting design must recognize and respond to the range of human visual and spatial needs and must grow from a synthesis of patterns of use, patterns of sunlight, visual requirements, and site-specific climate. The Novelty Hill–Januik Winery accomplishes this by creating an assembly of spaces in which the patterns of daylight and sunlight help meet the multifaceted needs of the owner and users.

AWARDS

» AIA Seattle Honor Award Commendation, 2009

» International Interior Design Association (IIDA)
Interior Design Award, 2008

» AIA Institute Honor Award for Interior Architecture, 2008

» WASLA Special Mention for Collaboration of Architecture
and Landscape Architecture, 2008

» IIDA Northern Pacific Chapter Awards, Hospitality Category, 2007

» Seattle Design Center's NW Design Awards,
Best of Contemporary Design, 2007

12

Center for Advanced Energy Studies

Exterior of south elevation. Photo:
C. Meek and K. Van Den Wymelenberg.

Interior, looking southeast from second floor
of atrium. Photo: C. Meek and K. Van Den
Wymelenberg.

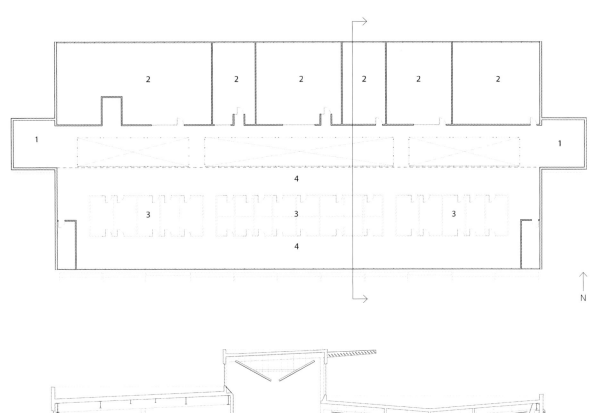

Center for Advanced Energy Studies
1 Atrium
2 Labs
3 Private Offices
4 Open Offices

N

THE CENTER FOR ADVANCED ENERGY STUDIES IS A JOINT PARTNERSHIP project of Idaho State University, Boise State University, the University of Idaho, and the Idaho National Laboratory. Researchers from each institution share office and lab space in the new facility adjacent to the Idaho National Laboratory's campus just north of downtown Idaho Falls. Representatives from each of these organizations held several project meetings before selecting a design and construction team and set several goals, including a building that would use 50 percent of the energy specified by the current energy code and utilize daylight as the primary light source for the overwhelming majority of the spaces. The project was executed through a design-build mechanism, and the contracted team was obligated to deliver upon these goals.

Idaho Falls is at the eastern edge of Idaho, about 100 miles west of Jackson, Wyoming. It is in the Snake River Plain and has a semiarid-cold high desert climate. The city has a relatively extreme climate, with wintertime high temperatures below freezing and frequent high winds, and summertime high temperatures above ninety degrees Fahrenheit with low relative humidity and cool nights. Space cooling drives a summer peak in energy use, and daylighting coupled with building shading and integrated lighting can provide significant relief during this period.

The narrow end of the long, two-story, steel frame structure rides the crest of the eastern bank of the Snake River. The building is long from east to west, with office spaces on both of the south-facing floor plates and laboratory spaces on the northern floor plates. A generous two-story atrium serves as the formal organizing element for the project and separates the office and laboratory zones within the building.

Interior, looking west from second floor of atrium. Photo: C. Meek and K. Van Den Wymelenberg.

Interior, looking southwest from second floor of atrium toward conference room. Photo: C. Meek and K. Van Den Wymelenberg.

Interior, looking southeast from catwalk in atrium. Photo: C. Meek and K. Van Den Wymelenberg.

Interior, looking west from first floor of atrium. Photo: C. Meek and K. Van Den Wymelenberg.

ATRIUM AND OFFICES

The two-story atrium defines the spatial organization of the building, running its entire length and capped with conference rooms at each end on the second level. Continuous clerestories facing north and south spill daylight onto sloped ceiling elements, highlighting the linearity of the space. On the south side of the second floor, open-plan office spaces project into the atrium and benefit from abundant diffuse daylight. The circulation way runs along the north side of the second level adjacent to the laboratories, to avoid blocking daylight access to the ground level. The ground floor of the atrium is a large, flexible-use area that serves as break-out space for informal meetings, lounge activities, and large community gatherings. The width of the atrium ensures that a significant amount of daylight reaches these ground-floor spaces as well. Light-colored walls and a translucent glass railing within the atrium serve as a balancing source of daylight for

the perimeter laboratory spaces through large interior viewing windows, maximizing the spatial effect of the daylight.

SHADING

In a high desert climate, shading the building during summertime is an essential aspect of daylighting design. In addition to shading from solar gain, glare control is also necessary. The building skin of the south facade is shaded with external devices, while internal light-redirecting surfaces minimize glare to the interior. Garth Shaw, of GSBS Architects, discussed the design approach to controlling the sun as a way of simultaneously adding to the overall aesthetic quality of the building. Designers also made a determined effort to see if the perimeter office spaces could be designed to function without the need for user-operated venetian blinds in the upper daylight window of the south facade so that the potential benefits of the daylighting design, including energy savings from dimming lights, could be realized. Too often, occupants lower blinds because of a short-term instance of glare and simply do not retract them. Therefore, the interior lightshelf is deep enough to block all direct sunlight and eliminate the need for blinds on the upper windows. Any direct sun passes over the top of the workstations and onto the wall at the back of the space without causing glare in the shared office area. The lower view windows below the lightshelf are fitted with louver blinds that help with glare control, while a compelling view of the Snake River encourages users to keep the blinds open if possible.

With only one row of perimeter open-plan office space, the overall shading and glare-control strategy is successful. The fixed exterior overhangs shade most of the glass during the hottest hours of the year, and the lightshelf and blinds on the view windows manage any remaining direct sun.

Even on the best projects, it is common for the users to have very little knowledge of the intent of the daylighting design or the solar-control strategy. The first year of occupancy is often the time to work through

this educational process. During this period, it became clear that while the shading elements and lightshelves worked well to keep most direct sun out of the space, veiling glare on computer screens still needed to be addressed. Therefore, louver blinds were introduced into the lower view windows; the upper daylight windows could function without blinds. These decisions resulted from dialogue between the building users, the facility staff, and the design team and represent a good example of the importance of this type of user understanding.

LABORATORIES

Laboratory spaces are notoriously difficult to daylight due to significant equipment and plumbing demands and the need to maximize the use of wall space for lab stations and cabinetry. Shaw discussed these challenges: "[Daylight] was a priority. The project team started with best-practice strategies in the office space and made fine adjustments to optimize the design. The labs were a whole different story. We had to carefully balance functional and configuration elements that create flexibility in the lab with daylighting elements. Overhead HVAC [heating, ventilation, and air-conditioning], lab gas, communication conduit, and other service carriers made toplighting impractical." Since the challenges of daylighting the laboratories from above proved too difficult, the laboratories were designed to be as narrow as was functional and were fitted with large north-facing windows. The designers kept the spaces narrow, to receive daylight from the north glazing, and opened up the ceilings to exposed piping and ducting, making them as high as possible for deeper daylight penetration. Additionally, large windows on the south wall provide some access to daylight from the atrium. More important, these relights create a sense of brightness and visual relief at the back of the space, reducing contrast from the northern sky, especially on overcast days.

AWARDS

» LEED Gold, 2009

» Mountain States Construction "Best of 09" Merit Award
for Higher Education/Research, 2009

» ABC Utah—Honorable Mention, Institutional over $5 Million, 2008

» AIA Utah Merit Award, 2008

Interior, looking east in second-floor laboratory.
Photo: C. Meek and K. Van Den Wymelenberg.

Interior, looking west in first-floor laboratory.
Photo: C. Meek and K. Van Den Wymelenberg.

13

"The daylight creates a sort of dynamism within a simple palette of materials."
—John Mihkels, Weinstein AIU

WEINSTEIN AIU. PROJECT LOCATION: FEDERAL WAY, WASHINGTON

Ron Sandwith EX3 Teen Center

Exterior view looking northwest.
Photo: C. Meek and M. Foley.

Gymnasium, looking north. Translucent skylights and clerestories illuminate the walls, floor, and ceiling for a balanced distribution of daylight. Photo: C. Meek and M. Foley.

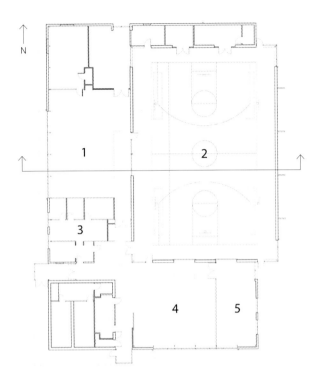

Ron Sandwith EX3 Teen Center

1 Classroom/Meeting Room
2 Gym
3 Administration
4 Game Room
5 Music Room

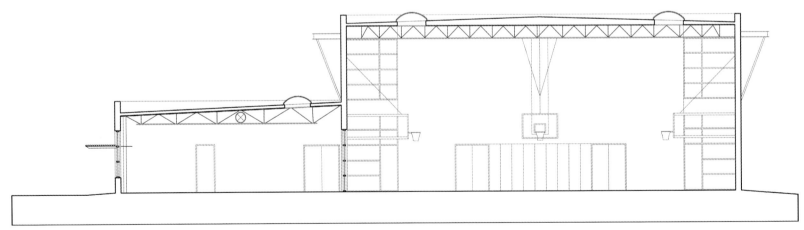

THE RON SANDWITH EX3 TEEN CENTER IS A BOYS & GIRLS CLUB SITED IN FEDeral Way, about twenty-five miles south of Seattle. It is dedicated entirely to teenage users and was the first of its kind for the Boys & Girls Club at a national level. The center is adjacent to an alternative high school and a Head Start facility, forming a small campus where each facility benefits from the resources of the others. The program consists of a large central gymnasium, a game room, a meeting room, staff offices with a reception area, and typical building support spaces such as restrooms, storage, and utility spaces. The EX3 Teen Center is heavily occupied throughout the day, making energy efficiency and daylit design a priority. The facility serves as the gymnasium for the alternative high school, a childcare facility, and a teen center and community gathering place after school hours.

The Boys & Girls Club prioritized a cost-effective, low-maintenance, and resilient facility that would be a welcoming after-school hangout for

Entry, looking east, with plywood skylight well in foreground. Photo: C. Meek and M. Foley.

Game room, looking east. The interior volume is illuminated from skylights, a view to the gym, a translucent wall, and south-facing windows. Photo: C. Meek and M. Foley.

Exterior sunshade and interior fabric lightshelf at south-facing windows. Photo: C. Meek and M. Foley.

Gymnasium, looking south.
Photo: C. Meek and M. Foley.

teens. The design team, led by Weinstein AIU, formulated a tectonic diagram opposing two rectangular concrete boxes connected by a lightweight steel structure and directly expresses these raw materials. The two concrete boxes form the gymnasium and utility core, while a classroom and a multipurpose space occupy the lightweight steel volumes. The spaces in the steel volumes are intended for variable activities, whereas the program within the concrete volumes is more permanent. The design meets the objectives of the Boys & Girls Club while creating an inspiring gathering space and has become the benchmark for subsequent facilities for this organization.

UTILITY, ECONOMY, DAYLIGHT

The visual experience at the EX3 Teen Center is defined by an economy of material and a restrained, direct architectural language. The philosophy

of the design team at Weinstein AIU is that "it would be unethical and irresponsible not to include daylight" in its projects. The designers also recognize that the muted quality and relative scarcity of daylight in the Pacific Northwest elevate its importance in their design lexicon. The quality of daylight over the course of the day is highly variable due to the region's weather patterns, and the designers realized that this drama is best showcased against the backdrop of a simple material palette. Spare formal and material expression supplies a muted canvas on which the patterns of daylight create a rich visual experience. At the EX3 center, the design team employed concrete, steel, translucent fiberglass, and selected elements of wood in a material palette that is austere yet maintains clarity of construction. The precast, tilt-up concrete panels draw on the vernacular craft tradition refined in the apple warehouses of eastern Washington. "The daylight creates a sort of dynamism within a simple palette of materials," says John Mihkels of Weinstein AIU.

Glazing in the project is not excessive but is carefully placed so that the light it delivers is visible on key surfaces. The glazing locations and material choices work together to connect the inside with the outside in terms of weather and patterns of daylight.

BUILDING ORGANIZATION

Formally, the building is designed as two boxes, one housing the gym and the other acting as a container for building support services, with spaces wrapping two sides of the gym volume to provide space for classrooms and the game room. Within this framework, there is a deliberate relationship between the daylight apertures, the interior surfaces of the space, and the quality of light needed to support the programmatic functions of each space. The team conceived the gymnasium as a light-filled central volume similar to an atrium and used diffuse skylights to illuminate the vertical

West classroom, looking south. Translucent skylights and a view to the gym balance daylight from the perimeter windows. Photo: C. Meek and M. Foley.

West classroom, looking southeast. Translucent skylights and a view to the gym balance daylight from the perimeter windows. Photo: C. Meek and M. Foley.

surfaces on both sides of the concrete wall panels, creating a sense of brightness in the gym and for the adjacent classrooms. Perimeter zones are illuminated with windows provided primarily for views to the outdoors, while the tilt-up concrete walls that divide the gymnasium and the back wall of the classroom are illuminated from both sides by translucent skylights. This strategy has a threefold benefit. First, faced with a very limited budget, the design team chose to maximize the visual impact of simple translucent skylights by positioning each to illuminate key vertical surfaces of the space, the upper walls, and the ceiling. The appearance of these high surfaces is crucial to the perception of brightness within any architectural volume. Second, this strategy provides luminosity on interior walls that balances daylight from perimeter view windows, thus minimizing brightness contrast. Third, this allows for an uncommon sense of transparency when moving from one space to the next and to the outdoors.

GYMNASIUM

The gymnasium fenestration is composed of four linear skylights and a combination of view windows and clerestories that are organized to join the "eroded" corners of the main tilt-up concrete box. The corner clerestories admit light onto each opposing wall, while the skylights fill in the gaps near the mid-span of the longitudinal wall surfaces and push light onto the floor in the middle of the space. The apertures are not large but are located such that they put the light immediately on vertical surfaces, which increases the perception of brightness despite their relatively small size. The view windows are positioned vertically in line with the clerestory windows so that the surfaces surrounding them are well illuminated, reducing perceived contrast and promoting a comfortable view to the exterior.

Detail at interior lightshelf and exterior overhang.
Photo: C. Meek and M. Foley.

MULTIPURPOSE SPACE AND CLASSROOMS

The active multipurpose space to the south and the quiet classroom to the west of the gymnasium are lightweight enclosures structured by metal studs, with open-web steel bar-joists, an exposed metal deck, and structural columns located inside the curtain-wall envelope. These spaces are designed to be more flexible and adaptable than the gym and are easily reconfigured for continuously changing uses, from games and dances to community meetings. The interior partitions are fitted with translucent fiberglass panels that help visually extend the classroom into the adjacent spaces and also provide vertical surfaces that glow with diffused daylight and increase spatial brightness. The carefully detailed curtain-wall at the west facade is fitted with an interior tension-mounted sailcloth lightshelf and an exterior metal louver shading device. Diffuse skylights deliver daylight to areas beyond the reach of the perimeter daylight zone.

MEASURING SUCCESS

The Seattle Daylighting Lab conducted extensive daylight studies exploring several design alternatives. The design team indicated that "the studies were invaluable in getting the owner to include daylight in the space. They were useful for making a design argument by backing it up with both subjective imagery and empirical performance data." The Boys & Girls Club was initially interested in the operational energy savings offered by integrated lighting controls and is now extremely happy with the quality of light in the spaces as well. The building has become the organization's baseline expectation for all new construction projects, and it continues to incorporate innovative designs in its structures. With the Ron Sandwith EX3 Teen Center, the success story began during construction, when the contractors were surprised to discover that there was very little need for job-site lighting because the daylight was sufficient for their work. User benefits and energy savings started immediately!

AWARDS

» AIA Honor Award, 2008
» PCI Design Award for Best Public Building, 2007

14

"The district was interested in doing something that pushed the limits of sustainable design . . . but at the same time, nothing was a given and each sustainable strategy of new technology needed to be well supported."

—David Mount, Mahlum

MAHLUM. PROJECT LOCATION: KIRKLAND, WASHINGTON

Ben Franklin Elementary School
Lake Washington School District

Exterior view at entry looking northwest.
Photo: C. Meek and K. Van Den Wymelenberg.

Classroom, looking east. An interior lightshelf controls direct sunlight from the upper window and redirects diffuse daylight to a sloped ceiling cloud. Photo: C. Meek and K. Van Den Wymelenberg.

Ben Franklin Elementary School,
Lake Washington School District
1 Classrooms
2 Art Room
3 Cafeteria
4 Gym
5 Administration
6 Library

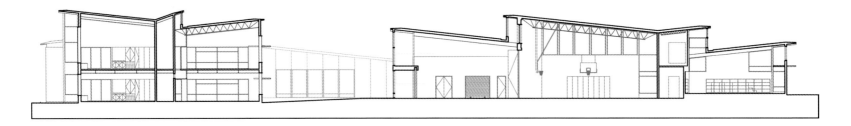

IN 2003, THE LAKE WASHINGTON SCHOOL DISTRICT SELECTED MAHLUM TO design a replacement for the aging Ben Franklin Elementary School in Kirkland, a forested urban community just to the east of Seattle. David Mount, the project architect at Mahlum, pointed out that "the district was interested in doing something that pushed the limits of sustainable design—they were a very receptive client in that sense . . . but at the same time, nothing was a given and each sustainable strategy or new technology needed to be well supported." There was some initial discussion about adopting California's Collaborative for High Performance Schools rating system for use in Washington. Together, Mahlum and the district decided to get aggressive about designing a more sustainable school well ahead of the state requirement that was eventually put in place, called Washington Sustainable Schools. Daylighting and natural ventilation were two significant design goals for this project. While the design team identified several reinforcing synergies between design demands for daylighting and natural ventilation, and the strategies it proposed had good general support from teachers, students, and the principal, the designers needed support from the building maintenance staff before they could implement these strategies. That is where the vision and leadership of Forest Miller, director of support services, proved crucial for the success of the project. Mount said, "When it came down to key decisions when certain design elements were maybe going to be removed . . . these kinds of decisions were really made by the facilities staff." It was Miller's commitment to realizing the project goals and his belief in the skills of the design team that ensured these strategies remained part of the project.

SITE DESIGN AND BUILDING FORM

The building form evolved from a series of goals and restrictions. Large areas of the site could not be used for the new building due to zoning limita-

Corridor at main entry with view to rain garden. Photo: C. Meek and K. Van Den Wymelenberg.

View to rain garden from corridor. Photo: C. Meek and K. Van Den Wymelenberg.

Courtyard rain gardens between classroom bars allow for daylight and views. Photo: C. Meek and K. Van Den Wymelenberg.

Exterior view of classroom wing looking east. Photo: C. Meek and K. Van Den Wymelenberg.

Opposite:

Daylight from two sides in a second-floor classroom. Photo: C. Meek and K. Van Den Wymelenberg.

Sliding transparent relight panels allow for visual brightness and views from the commons. Photo: C. Meek and K. Van Den Wymelenberg.

tions. It also had to be constructed around the existing school so that the transition to the new building would be seamless. These demands, combined with the narrow and asymmetrical site, meant that the new building had to be located entirely on one side of the site or the other. The district also had a prohibition against the use of skylights in any of its buildings, so vertical glass was the only means of providing daylighting. In addition to these restrictions, several goals further shaped the site and informed the building design. According to Mount, "The relationship between the buildings and the woods to the north needed to be very strong." The building was placed in proximity to the woods, affording ample view opportunities toward the north. The shared goal of achieving a sustainable design placed a high priority on daylighting and natural ventilation. Therefore, the spaces needed to be narrow and highly articulated in order to provide access to daylight from multiple sides and to outdoor air inlets and outlets. Essentially, the site restrictions combined with the priority for daylight, view, and

natural ventilation produced a highly articulated, two-story, courtyard layout in which several classrooms wrap indoor and outdoor shared spaces. A cluster of four classrooms encloses an indoor activity area with large north-facing windows, while groups of classrooms form outdoor courtyards.

After establishing this general site layout, the design team moved into schematic design stages for the building itself, which ended up as a series of connected buildings. The teachers requested that classrooms be as square as possible for space programming purposes, which presented challenges for both daylighting and natural ventilation because the spaces would be deeper than could be ventilated or daylit from one side. The formal articulation helped introduce daylight from multiple sides of the space and facilitated some cross ventilation; however, it did not provide sufficient daylight or airflow. Openings in the roof were necessary for introducing daylight to the portion of the classroom farthest from the windows and adequately ventilating the room, so the design team created a series of breaks in the roof that

Commons, looking west. This area is illuminated from a south-facing clerestory and tall, north-facing view windows. Photo: C. Meek and K. Van Den Wymelenberg.

Double-height art classroom, looking northeast. This classroom is illuminated from one side with overhead doors and clerestory glazing. Photo: C. Meek and K. Van Den Wymelenberg.

would accommodate clerestory windows. Mount said that team members spent a lot of time "looking at the roof forms to accommodate the passive design goals while at the same time considering the formal characteristics. Initially, the roof geometry did not have these breaks, and it took pulling them apart to provide the daylight and allow for the natural ventilation."

COURTYARDS, CLASSROOMS, AND ACTIVITY AREAS

Large outdoor courtyards organize the layout of the buildings, provide space for light and air, and supply a visible connection to the local ecology through a series of rain gardens. As users circulate through hallways, the gymnasium, and the library, there is consistent interplay between inside and outside, with physical access to courtyards and visual access through the courtyards to the forest beyond. Further enriching the relationship between indoors and outdoors, each classroom has a direct view to a garden space with an sophisticated designed landscape. Classrooms are organized in two-story clusters that line the north edge of the courtyards. In addition to opening onto the courtyards, each classroom opens onto a north-facing, shared, indoor activity area through large, glazed, sliding parti-

tions that provide access to additional daylight at the back of the classroom and offer views to the forest. The activity spaces also create a pathway for stack ventilation, by which warm air rises into the taller space and out of the building's operable outlets high in the activity space.

Each classroom has large clerestory windows to the south with view windows looking over the courtyard. There are large relight openings into the well-daylit activity space. Clerestory openings high in the classroom bring daylight onto the vertical surfaces of the upper portion of the north wall and balance brightness levels across the interior volume. Finally, several of the classroom spaces also have two outdoor walls with small windows in the second outdoor wall for both view and daylight.

The roof overhangs in the classrooms and activity areas were designed to minimize direct sun penetration during the hottest times of the year, entirely avoiding the need for refrigerant-based cooling. The roof overhangs are supplemented with fixed exterior window shading that minimizes glare and heat gain. These shading solutions proved equally valuable for the natural cooling system and promote visual comfort. Interior lightshelves placed below the clerestory windows on the south wall help redirect daylight toward the ceiling while also further reducing glare from direct sun

Multipurpose room, looking west. This area is illuminated from a north-facing clerestory and south-facing clerestory windows. Photo: C. Meek and K. Van Den Wymelenberg.

Library, looking west. Photo: C. Meek and K. Van Den Wymelenberg.

within the classrooms. The amount of window area in these classrooms is very similar to that found in typical classrooms in any contemporary school building. What makes these classrooms special is that the relationship between the glass and key interior surfaces is carefully designed to ensure a high-quality distribution of daylight.

LIBRARY, CAFETERIA, AND ART STUDIO

The larger shared spaces and classroom clusters use a similar architectural grammar, but each is modified to meet specific space needs. Generally, the library, cafeteria, and art studio have large shed roofs broken so as to provide daylight through tall clerestory windows.

The library has two generous south-facing clerestories, one at the perimeter and one that pours daylight onto its back wall. The very limited use of east- and west-facing glazing helps avoid glare. View windows are provided near the storytelling and reading room. The cafeteria necessitates a larger space with a deeper floor plate. Like the library, it has two clerestories, but these face north, with one at the perimeter and one near the back wall. The deeper floor plate and north-facing clerestories substantially increase the window area. Furthermore, large view windows are permitted on the north facade into the courtyard garden. When a movable partition between the gymnasium and the cafeteria is retracted, the rear clerestory admits light directly into the gymnasium. With the partition extended, as shown, daylight washes the partition and balances the brightness across the space. The art studio is comparatively simple and has a very narrow floor plate. It has only north glazing so as to provide even light for artwork. The glazing-to-floor-area ratio is very high, but in this case, the glazing is

Library, looking east from entry along clerestory monitor. Photo: C. Meek and K. Van Den Wymelenberg.

very much about providing a view to the large evergreen trees just outside the window. The top clerestory glazing is so high relative to the floor plate that it acts much like a skylight and distributes daylight from the brightest part of the sky toward the primary work surfaces.

AWARDS

» AIA Committee on Architecture for Education (CAE),
Educational Facility Design, Award of Excellence, 2007

» AIA Northwest and Pacific Region, Design Merit Award, 2007

» American Association of School Administrators (AASA),
Walter Taylor Award, 2007

» AIA Committee on the Environment (COTE),
Top Ten Green Projects, 2006

» AIA Seattle Honor Award for Washington Architecture, 2006

» AIA Washington Council Civil Design, Merit Award, 2006

» CEFPI Pacific Northwest Region, Award of Merit, 2006

» CEFPI International, Design Concept Award, 2004

15

"[Thiry's] designs emphasized economy, context, use of local materials, awareness of local light conditions, and integration of art and technological innovation."

—Barbara Johns, author of *Jet Dreams*

THE MILLER HULL PARTNERSHIP. PROJECT LOCATION: SEATTLE, WASHINGTON

Northeast Branch, Seattle Public Library

Exterior corner, looking northwest, with existing conifers. Photo: C. Meek and K. Van Den Wymelenberg.

Periodicals and reading room looking south. Computer workstations (at right) are illuminated by diffuse skylights from above and shielded from direct sun and glare by translucent panels. Photo: C. Meek and K. Van Den Wymelenberg.

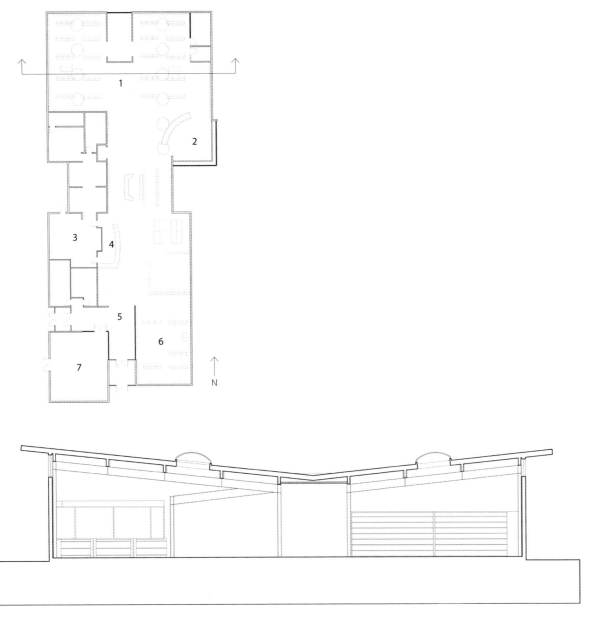

Northeast Seattle Branch Library

1 Book Stacks
2 Reading Area
3 Administration
4 Circulation Desk
5 Entry
6 Children's Section
7 Meeting Room

THE NORTHEAST BRANCH LIBRARY OF THE SEATTLE PUBLIC LIBRARY SYSTEM was originally constructed in 1953, designed by highly influential Seattle architect Paul Thiry. For nearly fifty years, this library, with its clean structural lines, broad eaves, expansive perimeter glazing, and deference to landscape, represented the classic characteristics of mid-century Northwest Modernism. Barbara Johns, author of *Jet Dreams: Art of the Fifties in the Northwest*, describes Thiry's work: "His designs emphasized economy, context, use of local materials, awareness of local light conditions, and integration of art and technological innovation, especially with concrete."[3] In 2003, the Seattle Landmarks Preservation Board designated the Northeast Branch Library a City of Seattle landmark.

From its initial construction, the library was subject to unusually high demand from the surrounding community and was second in circulation only to Seattle's Central Branch Library. In 1998, the Seattle Public Library system undertook a broad campaign to revitalize its network of branch libraries through a $196.4 million bond program, Libraries for All. The goal was to double the size of the library while respecting and preserving the character of the existing design. The Miller Hull Partnership was selected to design the addition and set forth with the goal of providing a high-quality library environment that achieved aggressive sustainability and energy-efficiency goals. Passive cooling, natural ventilation, and the use of daylight as the primary source of illumination were central to meeting these objectives.

The existing library sits on the corner of a north-south thoroughfare with its dominant public facade to the east. Due in part to the lack of available land adjacent to the site, the design team determined that the addition would create new building area to the north, extending the east- and west-facing facades. In order to meet solar-control and passive-cooling goals (and reduce heat loss in winter), the designers decided to minimize east- and west-facing glass and use just enough to meet ventilation requirements. Miller Hull was committed to the success of the passive systems, including daylighting, and worked with the Seattle Daylighting Lab to explore a range

Renovated 1953 Paul Thiry interior (now the children's section). Photo: C. Meek and K. Van Den Wymelenberg.

Junction of existing gable library massing and new butterfly roof. Photo: C. Meek and K. Van Den Wymelenberg.

of envelope concepts. Together, they devised an integrated toplighting and sidelighting strategy.

Deliberate space planning around patterns of daylight, sunlight, occupancy, and visual comfort criteria is a powerful tool in daylighting design. The Northeast Branch Library takes full advantage of this strategy and provides a carefully crafted set of luminous environments tailored to the activities that the spaces are designed to support. This takes the form of multiple layers of light and greater and lesser degrees of control tuned to the specific program elements of the library environment.

CENTRAL STACKS AND STUDY TABLES

The central book stack area is designed to support critical visual tasks such as reading, browsing for books, and using the quiet study tables. These tasks require consistent, diffuse ambient illumination and would be severely impaired by the presence of direct sunlight. The daylight distribution in this zone is highly controlled in both distribution and intensity. A series of carefully sized, circular, translucent skylights provides the primary layer of light. The skylights distribute even and relatively consistent diffuse daylight to the center of the library under sunny skies and maximize illumination levels under Seattle's dominant overcast sky condition. This strategy functions in several critically reinforcing ways. It produces sufficient illumination on the surfaces of the book stacks, which would otherwise be in deep shadow if lit from perimeter glazing. Furthermore, daylight washes the interior wall surfaces with diffuse light from the overhead sky dome, thus reducing the contrast between the interior surfaces and the relatively small perimeter windows. In turn, the perimeter clerestory windows illuminate the ceiling surface with daylight, reducing the contrast between the skylight apertures and the ceiling plane. These relationships maintain visual comfort in the space despite the highly variable availability of daylight throughout the year.

Looking northeast from circulation desk.
Photo: C. Meek and K. Van Den Wymelenberg.

Looking west from central reading area
toward stacks. Photo: C. Meek and K. Van
Den Wymelenberg.

Looking north at new butterfly roof with wood-
slat ceiling, new cylinder pendant fixture, and
daylit stacks to the east and west. Photo: C.
Meek and K. Van Den Wymelenberg.

Since the skylights are diffuse, this area remains free of direct sun that would impair visual tasks and add unnecessary heat load, diminishing the success of the passive cooling design.

COMMUNITY READING ROOM

The community reading room is designed to be a variable and dramatic space where direct sunlight and diffuse daylight mix, alternate, and interact with the seasons, weather, and time of day. The reading room is a flexible-use space. Users can choose to sit in direct sun, shade, or diffuse daylight, depending on their visual preference and specific visual needs. The space is illuminated by a high clerestory and an expanse of glass that provides a visual connection both into and out of the library at its most public facade. This glazing serves as a window to the community but might be a serious source of glare if it were not for the library's operation schedule. The space faces largely east, and the library typically opens at 10:30 A.M., so the majority of low-angle direct sunlight does not enter the space during its peak occupancy time. Organizing this program element to the east side of the new building helps avoid glare while maintaining comfortable views to the exterior.

A set of public use computer terminals adjoins the community reading room. These workstations are in a fixed location, giving users little alternative if glare is present, so it is of paramount importance to ensure visual comfort at all times. Despite the challenges posed by the workstations' fixed positions and their proximity to the dynamic reading room, designers achieved persistent visual comfort by means of a curved translucent panel that shields computer users from contrast and uncontrolled direct sunlight and eliminates any direct line of sight to the disc of the sun. Ambient daylight washes the translucent panel from above via diffuse skylights in the adjacent book stacks area and supplies general illumination. At night, the panel serves as a projection screen for a luminous art installation.

Translucent circular skylights provide ambient daylight illumination between book stacks and on primary vertical surfaces. Photo: C. Meek and K. Van Den Wymelenberg.

CIRCULATION DESK

In any library, the design and ergonomics of the circulation desk are a primary concern. An important part of the design is lighting. Saddled with the most demanding visual comfort criteria, this space is occupied at all times and serves as both a transaction counter and the stage for interaction between library staff and patrons. The Seattle Daylighting Lab has consulted on a wide range of library daylighting projects and discovered through that experience that librarians' number one complaint about their visual comfort conditions is glare from low-angle direct sun at the circulation desk. The design team deemed it crucial to ensure that the librarians at the circulation desk never experience direct line of sight to the disc of the sun. Partly for this reason, the circulation desk was tucked into the connecting space between the existing library and the new addition. This area is characterized by darker surface finishes and electric task illumination, which ensure a consistent luminous environment despite changing sky conditions or sun position.

INTEGRATION WITH ELECTRIC LIGHTING

Although daylight is the dominant source of illumination in the Northeast Branch Library, electric lighting plays a crucial role. People are often surprised when they walk into a building and the electric lights are off, even if there is a more than sufficient level of daylight illumination. It may be part of cultural expectations that the lights are on when a place is open. For this reason, the careful inclusion of electric accent lighting can provide sparkle and focus, giving users a sense that the space is open and that the light is indeed coming from somewhere. It can also help users accept reduction or elimination of ambient electric light output when daylight is present by providing a visual anchor to the space. This strategy is deployed in the community reading room, where the glow of a small set of custom blown-glass accent fixtures signals that the library is open for business, while daylight provides the ambient illumination.

The experience of the library at night is dramatically different than during daylight hours. During the day, most electric light sources are controlled off. At night, the central stacks and reading room are illuminated solely by stack lights that have had the top of the fixture removed to create an indirect up-lighting component. This gives the space an intimate scale, as the vertical surfaces and the ceiling recede and the stack surfaces become the primary luminous entities. Table lamps supplement lower ambient nighttime light levels when needed for reading.

Electric light sources also serve as a unifying feature that ties the new addition to the existing library volume day and night. A single row of glowing cylinders runs the entire length of the library in relief against the wooden ceiling slats, connecting the existing and new portions of the building.

The visual experience of the Northeast Branch Library shifts with the rhythm of light offered by the site and the sky, revealing the patterns of light generated by the connection between space and the passage of time. This creates a unique duality between night and day in which the sky provides the dominant source of illumination during daylight hours but the creative use of electric lighting and dark adaptation allows for lower illumination levels during evening hours, evoking a more intimate and dramatic setting that captures the spirit of the night.

Designing with the Light of Place

Lessons Learned

ARCHITECTURAL FORMS IN AND OF THEMSELVES CREATE LUMINOUS CONDI-
tions. Effective building design uses daylight in a way that promotes rather than hinders design goals. Although daylighting design elements and geometric relationships will vary from place to place in response to the specifics of a particular site and climate, practitioners can employ conceptual approaches to daylighting that are rooted in the visual, spatial, and experiential needs of building inhabitants everywhere. In this spirit, we offer lessons learned from our experience in the Pacific Northwest that we believe transcend the specificity of a particular building type or regional context. The following strategies are meant to enable designers to deploy geometric daylighting design principles within a conceptual framework that addresses the needs of building owners and occupants while meeting experiential goals and to help designers become more aware of the luminous environment created by their design choices.

1   Set design criteria and test design decisions.

2   Put daylight where it is most needed.

3   Focus first on spatial distribution of light, then foot-candles.

4   Understand the implications of daylight variability and patterns of occupancy.

5   Bring in light from above whenever possible.

6   Consider occupant behavior carefully and realistically, especially when selecting window coverings.

7   Use interior finishes to shape perceptions of brightness and darkness.

8   Use the sequence of movement through space to set the stage for desired visual experiences.

9   Integrate electric lighting into the *dynamic* scene.

10 Address whole building energy performance through integrated design.

Practical Considerations

SET DESIGN CRITERIA AND TEST DESIGN DECISIONS

Daylighting criteria will vary from space to space based on design goals and visual tasks. The designer plays a critical role in developing criteria that are appropriate to visual comfort, patterns of occupancy, times of use, and the locally specific availability of daylight. Assigning daylighting and electric lighting illuminance goals, direct sunlight tolerance, and views criteria to each of the project's specific program elements is a crucial first step. This should include setting priority for spaces where daylight is critical, merely desired, unimportant, or detrimental. It may include Leadership in Energy and Environmental Design (LEED) or other building rating system criteria; however, it should be stressed that successful daylighting requires a deep understanding of the visual experience that transcends any single metric.

One method used to ensure the appropriate application of this principle in the design process is to create a daylight programming document that establishes priorities for daylight, views, and tolerance for direct sunlight before schematic design at the outset of preliminary building organization. Typically, designers would prioritize daylight and views in areas that are most heavily occupied for extended periods of time, including critical visual task areas such as offices or other continuously occupied spaces. Areas such as corridors, aisle ways, or flexible-use gathering spaces can tolerate direct sunlight, whereas fixed workstations or reception desks will rarely remain comfortable in direct sun. Key questions to answer for each major program element and the discrete spaces within them include the following: *Is daylight important for this space? Are views to the exterior important? How frequently is this space used? What time of day and time of year will the space be occupied? How crucial is the control of direct sun and glare? What is the minimum design illumination? Are there maximum light levels allowable? What is the ideal solar orientation of particular program elements given its time of use and visual comfort criteria? What might be a good strategy (sidelighting, toplighting) for providing, or not providing, daylight in each particular space given other known factors such as adjacency, size, and the shape of the room?* These questions form the basis for identifying design goals and testing ideas through simulation in order to ensure that a proposed design meets previously determined objectives.

All of the daylighting design ideas represented in this book are the result of extensive simulation and testing of architectural design alternatives. The establishment of criteria creates a benchmark by which to evaluate the performance of a given design option. Testing design decisions requires an understanding of both the patterns of diffuse illumination and exposure to direct sunlight within a space. Times and locations of direct sunlight patterns can be understood quickly with any design software that allows for simple shadow casting, while daylighting simulation software or physical models can identify the distribution of *diffuse* daylight. The process of testing design alternatives yields knowledge, provides guidance, and generates new questions that might otherwise have remained unexamined. It should be noted that visual comfort performance is only a consideration for times when the building is occupied. Studying the relationship between occupied times and patterns of sunlight can foster useful design opportunities.

With a clear description of the performance of a space within the building in hand, the designer must synthesize the luminous and spatial needs of the program elements with the space planning and workstation configuration relative to the established design criteria.

PUT DAYLIGHT WHERE IT IS MOST NEEDED

It sounds so simple that it should go without saying, but it is crucial to identify where daylight is most valuable and to focus design attention on creating the opportunity for it to be present in these areas. Unlike criteria setting, this objective stresses creating a design process that focuses on the primary space type included in the building. The quantity and distribution of daylight illuminance relative to the visual tasks and experiences within a building provide exceptional form-giving opportunities. A common example of this is providing higher levels of daylight illuminance in classrooms or office areas rather than in adjacent circulation ways or entrance lobbies. This approach reflects the economy of providing the daylight resource where visual tasks demand it, which is where occupants spend the majority of their time (classrooms or workstations), versus areas that require lower light levels and are used in a more informal and transitory manner (corridors and circulation ways). It may be tempting to lavish design attention on one-off or signature elements such as an entry lobby, yet the greatest challenge in designing fundamentally daylit buildings lies in the design innovation required to provide broad access to high-quality daylight and views within the spaces where building occupants spend the vast majority of their time.

FOCUS FIRST ON SPATIAL DISTRIBUTION OF LIGHT, THEN FOOT-CANDLES

Daylight is often most suited to being a source of *ambient* illumination, light that is used for general space lighting. Typically, this means putting light on the walls, ceiling, and key architectural surfaces in order to define the visual experience, support way-finding and circulation, and supply sufficient lighting for general vision. In most cases, after a minimum threshold of illuminance is met, say twenty foot-candles of general horizontal illumination, what matters most in terms of lighting quality are the brightness relationships on key surfaces throughout the space. An effective design includes a compositional hierarchy of lighter and darker surfaces and places daylight apertures and primary surfaces in proximity to one another so that the desired composition is met through time and across predominant sky conditions. This is particularly important when dealing with view windows and other daylight apertures that are in the immediate visual field. For example, in a space illuminated from windows on one side, the most critical surface for daylight illumination is often the wall opposite the windows. If its brightness is created by daylight, the contrast between the perimeter windows and the interior surface opposite these windows will nearly always be balanced.

Our experience shows that when the contrast relationships between key surfaces achieve harmonious composition, the importance of horizontal daylight illuminance is diminished. This concept is analogous to indirect lighting in electric lighting design, which focuses attention on the ceiling plane and key vertical surfaces rather than the task plane exclusively, resulting in higher occupant satisfaction, even with lower light levels. It may not be a coincidence that much of the movement toward indirect lighting occurred in office buildings where daylight was no longer a primary source of illumination. As we see a reemergence in the use of daylight, we are discovering that daylight can be the primary source of ambient illumination, while electric lighting is best suited to providing consistent task lighting in key areas when needed.

UNDERSTAND THE IMPLICATIONS OF DAYLIGHT VARIABILITY AND PATTERNS OF OCCUPANCY

The primary challenge of designing for daylight lies in addressing its variability. Daylight, sunlight, and sky conditions are changing almost constantly. The relationship between those changes and patterns of building occupancy is critical in effective daylighting design. Aligning building organization with expected periods of use, especially coordinating occupancy times with the patterns of direct sunlight, is a key design opportunity. In this respect, it is incumbent on the designer to make an intentional and informed decision regarding the degree of tolerance or desirability of changes in light intensity, patterns of sunlight, and distribution of diffuse daylight at different locations within a building. Some spaces, such as lobbies, corridors, and flexible-use spaces, are ideally suited to the dramatic presence of direct sun of varying angles and wide fluctuations in illumination ranges across the period of a day. For this reason, they do not require a strict response to solar geometry. Others, such as fixed office workstations and transaction counters, require a continuous and high level of control throughout their periods of use and there-

fore must be shaped to take advantage of the most consistent distributions of light from the sun and sky. Architectural form, orientation, and materiality are at the core of shaping patterns of light over time.

The design of the Seattle Central Library by the Office for Metropolitan Architecture (OMA) illustrates this principle. Rather than carefully controlling the visual experience based on tasks at specific locations, the OMA design creates a wide range of conditions and offers users the flexibility to choose the settings that best fit their current needs. In this regard, a seat on the east side of the reading room (the "Living Room") might be well suited for working on a laptop during an overcast day at 2 P.M., though on a cool sunny day at 10 A.M. with direct beam sunlight, it might be better suited for informal conversation with a friend over coffee.

The strategy of creating a range of possible visual experiences can work well for nonspecific-use spaces in a library of this scale. It is, however, less successful with many of the fixed workstations, such as reference desks, some of which had to be relocated, in part due to unmitigated glare. Glare is also a reoccurring problem for some of the public-access computer terminals and private offices. However, fittingly, the majority of these functions are located in the center of the library, in an area called the "Mixing Chamber," where the extreme variability of the perimeter zones has been replaced with uniform overhead electric lighting and complete elimination of all direct sunlight.

BRING IN LIGHT FROM ABOVE WHENEVER POSSIBLE

Diffuse daylight from overhead consistently delivers both effective ambient illumination and user satisfaction. By enabling an even, consistent distribution of horizontal illumination and the ability to wash interior vertical surfaces with diffuse light, toplighting affords unmatched performance. The reasons for this are twofold. The first is the nature of the sky. In overcast-sky climates, the brightest part of the sky is directly overhead (at the zenith), and in clear-sky climates, the roof receives more hours of direct solar exposure than does any other orientation. The second, and perhaps the greatest reason for the effectiveness of toplighting, is that toplighting often enables the segmentation of views and daylight. This means that if occupants close the window shades on their view windows due to low-angle sunlight or the need for privacy, they will not disable the daylight from overhead apertures. Additionally, daylight provided from diffuse overhead apertures enables an even distribution of horizontal illumination across a large area and the ability to wash vertical surfaces with light, with relatively little variability in distribution across time. This bodes well for the integration of electric light fixtures, since the patterns of daylight from above are often very similar to the distribution of electric light output. It should be noted that toplighting often has the greatest potential for heat gain during the summer and heat loss during the winter through glazing. However, it is often possible to provide effective daylight from above with much less glass area than most vertical glazing configurations. As always, these factors must be considered within the context of overall project goals.

CONSIDER OCCUPANT BEHAVIOR CAREFULLY AND REALISTICALLY, ESPECIALLY WHEN SELECTING WINDOW COVERINGS

As architects and owners strive to create higher-performing buildings, the role of occupant behavior becomes increasingly crucial. Architects can design buildings with the potential for effective daylight performance, but realizing performance expectations requires users to operate the building in the intended manner. This is particularly true with regard to window shades and blinds. It is common to find buildings with extensive glazing in which occupants have drawn all of the blinds in an effort to control glare. Sometimes this is because the designer has not considered low sun angles or other glare sources, but often it is simply that the range of sky conditions and seasonal sun angles is too broad to be managed with fixed architectural elements. Because of this, and because of the need to satisfy all occupants across all times, blinds are installed and are often positioned for worst-case conditions, essentially defeating the intent of the daylighting design. Manually operated blind systems are very effective if properly used; however, they require continuous user attention if they are to maintain complete glare control while achieving maximum daylight performance.

Automated glare control has the advantage of being deployed in response to specific sky conditions on an as-needed basis and can be retracted without user intervention when direct sunlight or glare is no longer present, thus allowing for unimpeded diffuse daylight. In most cases, this will deliver longer periods of effective daylight contribution, increased lighting energy savings, and longer durations of unobstructed views to the exterior. In some regards, however, automated shading acts as a blunt instrument. In working to entirely eliminate potential glare, many of these systems block all direct sunlight from entering the interior. This means that if a user enjoys the play of direct sun within his or her work area, that person will have to override the system. Furthermore, this type of glare-control system can conflict with passive solar-gain strategies during colder months. Designers considering automated glare-control and solar-shading systems must carefully determine where continuous sun control is necessary and where the play of sunlight is acceptable or beneficial to the interior quality of a space. Both automated and manual blinds can be very effective, depending on occupant preference and culture. An understanding of these variables and likely occupant behavior is key to designing comfortable interior environments with persistent daylight performance over time.

Designers may also find it necessary to take a proactive approach to educating users about the intent of the daylighting and solar-control systems, regardless of how simple or complex, preferably during the first year of occupancy. Even on the best projects, users commonly have little knowledge of the daylighting design intent or the solar-control strategy.

USE FINISHES TO SHAPE PERCEPTIONS OF BRIGHTNESS AND DARKNESS

The placement and composition of interior surface finishes and their reflectance value can be a powerful tool in shaping perception of brightness and darkness. It is commonly understood that high levels of reflectance (as in light-colored surfaces, not necessarily highly specular [shiny] surfaces) increase overall horizontal illuminance. The role that light-colored surface finishes can play in the management of contrast and perceived distribution of daylight luminance is less recognized. These finishes can be valuable in two places: on the surfaces surrounding windows and on vertical surfaces opposite perimeter glazing and directly adjacent to skylights. Views through windows tend to be substantially brighter than the interior surfaces adjacent to the windows. Reflective interior surface finishes at these locations can further diffuse daylight and reduce contrast between interior surfaces and the views beyond. Walls opposite perimeter glazing can be ideal for balancing brightness from these windows. Designers may specify a light-colored surface for the back wall or ceiling plane in order to ensure that light and dark surfaces are well composed across the section of a space. This is especially valuable when illuminating an interior from one side. Designers can amplify this effect by surrounding key light-colored surfaces with somewhat darker finishes so that the contrast creates the perception of additional brightness on the most critical surfaces.

USE THE SEQUENCE OF MOVEMENT THROUGH SPACE TO SET THE STAGE FOR DESIRED VISUAL EXPERIENCES

Designers have an opportunity to shape building users' perceptions of brightness by adjusting light levels through the sequence of movement through a building. This can be a powerful tool in transitioning from a bright exterior into an interior environment. In spaces that are well daylit during daylight hours, interiors tend to be illuminated at 1 to 3 percent of the available outdoor illumination. This often leads to a jarring transition, as the interior feels dark regardless of the actual illumination level while the eye adjusts to lower interior light levels. One way to design for this transition is to create an entry sequence that allows occupants to adjust gradually to low interior light levels as they move through circulation ways. Through this experience, the destination within the building, if it is well daylit, will feel substantially brighter than the relatively dark circulation ways.

Alvar Aalto used this principle to great effect in his iconic Mount Angel Abbey Library in Oregon. The sectional forms guide users from the entrance and through a masterful sequence of momentary spatial light reductions that sets the tone for contemplation and meditation. In the time it takes to walk from the approach beneath a canopy of trees, under the covered portico, through the lobby, and to the lending desk, visitors' eyes have time to dilate, and the whole of the visual system has adapted to the space's lower interior light levels. When visitors finally step down into the main reading spaces and move from the low rectilinear forms to vast vertical and curvilinear forms, they experience the rather minimal and muted daylight more viscerally. Although they physically descend through this sequence, they have the sensation of being lifted up visually by the daylight, which accentuates the bodily decompression to the larger architectural volume at the end of the sequence.

INTEGRATE ELECTRIC LIGHTING
INTO THE *DYNAMIC* SCENE

While automated or manual control of lighting is imperative in order to ensure substantial lighting energy savings (we routinely see 70 percent reductions in lighting energy use), there are richer opportunities for electric lighting design in the context of daylit buildings. The dynamic shifts in brightness and distribution from daytime to night in a daylit space offer the potential to embrace the day-night cycle by designing the electric lighting around a nighttime scene. This might be more intimate and more dramatic and, yes, might result in lower illuminance compared to using electric lighting as the primary source of illumination during all hours. Because of dark adaptation, humans expect and request less light at night. Much of our contemporary built environment has been designed to provide continuous, static electric lighting levels. We think that there is an enormous untapped potential for adaptable electric lighting design that is suited to its surroundings, that truly embraces daylight and the light-dark cycle to yield more comfortable, interesting, appropriate, and energy-efficient lighting.

Effective design of photo-responsive control systems must include an assessment of how various states of control affect the overall composition of light in the scene and, most critically, how users will perceive the transitions from electric illumination to daylight illumination. Many lighting-control systems that meet objective foot-candle criteria have been disabled because they produce unexpected and jarring transitions from day to night or under varying daylight conditions. In this regard, meeting energy-conservation goals is wholly contingent on creating high-quality distribution of daylight and electric light and choreographing the interplay of the two. Daylight tends to be more effective as an ambient illumination source despite its variability, while electric lighting is better applied to provide constancy and fixed points of focus. Our cultural expectations about interior spaces often include focal points of electric lighting. Where the ambient electric lighting is expected to be off much of the day, we often recommend the inclusion of decorative or accent lighting or wall washing with electric lighting in order to give depth and focus to the scene and to give occupants the sense that a space is open and active. In our experience, a seamless and gradual transition from daylight to electric light creates the most satisfying environment for occupants and is most effective at achieving energy savings.

ADDRESS WHOLE BUILDING ENERGY PERFORMANCE
THROUGH INTEGRATED DESIGN

For daylight to be designed into buildings in a sustainable manner, it must serve the visual comfort needs of people *and* substantially reduce energy consumption. The challenge is that it can do both or neither, and it takes skill to navigate the design and occupancy process so that the building achieves both over time. We often promote daylight as the meeting place for architects, engineers, building owners, and users because it is so tangible and important to each of these groups.

6 A.M. dark.

7 A.M. task and accent lighting.

8 A.M. ambient electric light with accent lighting.

Environments in which daylight is the primary source of illumination will change dramatically through time. Electric lighting should reflect this dynamism and flexibility in order to ensure both visual comfort and energy efficiency. Photos show the open office area at the University of Washington Integrated Design Lab in Seattle as daylight and electric light change throughout the day. Photos: C. Meek.

10 A.M. ambient daylight.

1 P.M. ambient daylight with task lamp.

3 P.M. ambient daylight with sunlight.

4 P.M. ambient daylight with line-of-sight to the solar disc.

5 P.M. twilight with task and accent lighting.

6 P.M. dark.

When considering the energy performance of the whole building, the goal of the daylight design is, at minimum, to provide sufficient illumination in order to minimize reliance on electric lighting, provide adequate building shading so as to minimize heat gain, and integrate these effects into the building engineering so that the structure requires smaller cooling systems thanks to reduced heat gain from glazing and electric lights. This is a basic example of the integrated design process, which is commonly defined as the synthesis of climate, use, loads, and systems for the purpose of creating a more comfortable and productive environment and a building that is more energy efficient than current best practices.[1] This process is likely to include an examination of the interactive effects of heating, cooling, and lighting factors associated with daylighting design decisions through both daylight testing and energy simulation. It will ensure that the design includes the amount of glass appropriate to meet daylighting demands yet avoids detrimental heat transfer or glare. We have found that the robust inclusion of daylight can save energy in any climate; however, there is always a balance between providing sufficient daylight for visual needs and energy use. It is often impossible to optimize for both; thus, value judgments are required.

We believe that daylight and views are a minimum requirement for humane architecture,[2] and therefore our recommendation is to ensure that the daylight design is satisfactory for people, even if it is not perfectly optimized for energy performance. In the quest to reduce reliance on electric lighting, we see the provision of high-quality daylit environments as a precursor to meeting aggressive energy-performance goals, since dissatisfied occupants are unlikely to accept automated control of electric light sources, meaning that limited or no energy savings will be realized. The purpose of buildings is to support human activity and create places that enrich our lives. We see daylight as fundamental to fulfilling the highest aspirations for both energy efficiency and environmental quality in the built environment.

LOOKING FORWARD

As we consider the future of building design and the value of daylight within it, it is important to revisit the purpose of architecture in our social framework. We build buildings to serve human activity, to provide places for learning, to foster enjoyment and creativity, and to support a wide range of productive pursuits. These priorities must remain paramount as we strive for increasingly efficient use of limited energy resources. We believe that the provision of daylight in buildings is central to all of these objectives and can also support reduced energy consumption. With organizations such as the U.S. Green Building Council promoting the use of daylight for improved indoor environmental quality and with the American Institute of Architects and the American Society of Heating, Refrigerating, and Air-Conditioning Engineers (ASHRAE) adopting the goal of designing only net-zero-energy buildings by the year 2030, it would seem that the use of daylight in buildings is here to stay. Yet, despite the recent reawakening to the beneficial impact of daylighting on the experiences of building occupants and evidence that daylight can reduce lighting energy use, an undertow is beginning to form that may jeopardize its resurgent status in our built environment.

Energy codes are often referred to as the "stick," and self-imposed standards and aggressive energy design goals are referred to as the "carrot." As approaches, both the stick and the carrot have the potential to improve energy performance in buildings and promote the role of daylight in accomplishing this goal. Surprisingly, both threaten the role of daylight in buildings. Building code–development bodies and others seeking to improve energy efficiency in buildings are crafting prescriptive standards that target window apertures as a liability and seek to substantially lower window area in new buildings as a surefire way of minimizing heating and cooling requirements.

It is interesting to note that the pursuit of aggressive energy-performance goals, such as the desire to create buildings that use no more energy than they produce on an annual basis, as promoted by the Living Building Challenge (LBC), can lead to the significant reduction or elimination of windows and skylights. Those seeking to achieve the goals of the LBC often meet energy requirement through photovoltaic arrays on the roof and the skin of a building. This often requires that energy production technology occupy a substantial proportion of the roof and skin, making less area available for skylights and windows and therefore daylight and views to the exterior.

As already discussed, before the availability of mechanical thermal and visual comfort systems, buildings were daylit out of necessity for the performance of basic visual tasks and required windows for access to fresh air. In these buildings, occupants dealt with technical issues of excessive heat transfer and glare with storm windows, shutters, curtains, and other means of maintaining comfort. By the middle of the twentieth century, improved mechanical systems enabled buildings to meet the minimum requirements for light and air without windows. When the initial wave of energy codes emerged in the 1970s, spurred by the 1973 oil embargo, windows came to be viewed as a liability because they contributed to heat gain and heat loss. This ultimately created a design culture in which daylight no longer factored into the architecture in a material way. We currently face this same threat from well-intentioned energy-efficiency policies.

With the advent of the sustainable design movement, we are beginning to relearn how to introduce daylight in order to connect humans with the natural rhythms of light and save energy while doing so. As we have discussed, building codes are promoting a simplistic approach to saving energy by mandating smaller windows that minimize thermal transfer. Ironically, energy codes could once again push daylight out of buildings!

When daylight is considered nothing more than an energy-efficiency measure, it can be erroneously cast in simple terms of cost-benefit on an energy-performance scale. It is unlikely that there is a clear, singular ideal point for most climates at which daylight and energy performance find a natural balance in terms of both energy efficiency and user preference. In order to meet our primary responsibility of creating high-quality indoor environments, we must develop a more complete understanding of the human experience within the built environment. The value of health, learning, and productivity outcomes must be demonstrably quantified and eloquently qualified so that they can be meaningfully factored into building design decisions. The recent emergence of photobiology as a field of scientific inquiry supports the belief that this critical understanding is in its infancy. It is imperative that architects and building owners participate in the development and application of this research, since this type of knowledge will allow the design profession to communicate its true value to society through an empirical understanding of the broader outcomes of good design (and may, in part, begin to insulate the profession from the boom-and-bust cycle of speculative real estate development).

Even with intentional development of the qualitative and quantitative valuation of the effects of daylight on human health and productivity, technological advances will continue to drive the transformation of daylighting design in architectural practice. More complex glass types and facade assemblies are under continuous development. We are likely to find increased adoption of dynamic building envelope strategies. These may free designers from having to choose between the need to provide solar shading and maintain diffuse daylighting and the desire to allow for light and views during the day and reduce the nighttime heat loss that occurs in static building systems. Environmentally responsive facade systems, including automated shading devices, and switchable glazing that can respond to weather conditions and sun positions can allow for appropriately sized daylight apertures while eliminating much of the thermal penalties.

These strategies combined with considerations of patterns of occupancy may enable us to create a building envelope that is optimized for human comfort when occupants are present and optimized for thermal efficiency when they are not. Electric lighting systems that use far less energy than in the past are also being rapidly engineered. Paradoxically, this reduces the total lighting energy that can be saved through the use of daylight and controls. However, the reduction of building loads across the board may actually increase the percentage of energy that can be saved through the use of daylight.

Given that technological advancement will certainly shape the design of daylight in buildings, some caution is warranted. For example, one of the purposes of dynamic facades is to moderate the sometimes extreme variability of daylight over time. Automated systems that are focused on managing environmental variability and glare from direct sunlight can conversely diminish the pleasure afforded by the accidental play of light and space that occurs in less controlled environments. Unquestioning adoption of these technologies could result in buildings that unwittingly impede a human connection with the built environment by eliminating a daily pattern of occupant interaction with the architecture and the outdoors. Despite the promise of increased building automation, we feel that an empowered, educated, and motivated building occupant who takes responsibility for his or her interior environment is the state of the art in building controls. Many questions are likely to emerge in the course of identifying the role of human behavior in building performance within the context of more technological or dynamically responsive buildings. Maybe building occupants will find pleasure and meaning in a deeper engagement with the built environment? Maybe advances in daylighting, human biological, and human social research will provide important psychophysical or psychosocial insights that can guide technological advancement? Maybe there are very simple solutions that resonate with basic human physical needs and can connect people with the outdoors as well as save energy? Maybe building owners or business owners might even seek to develop flexible work schedules that align patterns of occupancy with the optimum performance of their buildings and daylight hours? Maybe building inhabitants will demand more from their buildings and expect operable windows that offer substantial access to light and air? We face the very real challenge of meeting our energy-efficiency goals while creating buildings that provide healthy, high-quality interior environments in which people can live, work, and play. In meeting this goal, it is imperative that we include the most basic requirement of responsible architecture: daylight and a view to the outside world.

Pacific Northwest Daylighting Lab Network
Tools and Methods

THE PACIFIC NORTHWEST DAYLIGHTING LAB NETWORK TAKES AN ACTIVIST role both within the academy and the profession. The labs in the network have sought to develop partnerships with leaders in the Pacific Northwest design and engineering communities with the intention of fostering a hybrid research and practice model that promotes both energy efficiency and improved environmental quality. Daylighting touches nearly all aspects of building design, including building envelope, structure, materiality, mechan-ical systems, lighting systems, window coverings, and furnishings. For this reason, it does not currently fall squarely within the purview of any of the traditional disciplines associated with the design of buildings. This opening in the design process offers an opportunity for academics to engage with designers and building owners on issues of daylighting, solar shading, and other facets of climate-responsive design.

The Lab Network consists of university-operated facilities in urban cen-ters of the Pacific Northwest. Currently these include labs at the University of Washington in Seattle, the University of Oregon in Eugene and Portland, the University of Idaho in Boise, Washington State University in Spokane, and Montana State University in Bozeman. This network has emerged from a tradition of professional-academic collaboration on lighting and energy effi-ciency in buildings in the region's schools of architecture dating back roughly forty years. In the late 1990s, utilities in the Pacific Northwest partnered through the Northwest Energy Efficiency Alliance (NEEA) to foster the adop-

Real-time collaboration and performance feedback with the design team using a physical model in the mirror-box sky. Photo: J. Loveland.

Solar shading studies using a heliodon. Photo: C. Meek.

DESIGN GUIDANCE AND CRITERIA DEVELOPMENT

A primary task of the labs is to help architects set daylighting design goals and test design decisions. Setting appropriate daylighting design criteria and developing an understanding of site context are key elements at this stage of a project. Daylighting performance targets are both qualitative and quantitative and require collaboration with the architect, lighting designer, and practitioners in engineering disciplines. In building design, daylighting traditionally encompasses three primary avenues of inquiry: (1) aperture and interior surface design for effective and appropriate luminous distribution and intensity, (2) shading for glare control, and (3) shading for solar heat gain control. The interrelationships of these goals are complex and may, at times, be at cross purposes, which makes the establishment of project priorities at the outset of design critical to success.

A common first step in any lab project is to meet with the design team, consultants, and owner so that all parties understand and contribute to developing daylighting design goals. The design team develops the site context for daylighting by analyzing weather data and assessing site-specific overshadowing from adjacent vegetation, buildings, and landforms. Weather data can provide cloud cover percentages, likely exterior horizontal illuminance ranges, incident solar radiation, and the relationship between outdoor air temperature and solar geometry. The labs frequently use software tools such as Climate Consultant developed at the University of California, Los Angeles; the Energy Plus Weather File database of the U.S. Department of Energy; and custom spreadsheets Lab Network developed to assist designers in compiling these data.

Concurrently, the team establishes criteria for the project's interior spaces. First, designers establish minimum horizontal illuminance levels for program elements based on expected visual task requirements. Performance targets for daylighting include meeting sufficient illuminance targets over time, which contributes toward substantial electric lighting power savings. The usual minimum goals for daylight illuminance are that daylight

tion of energy-conservation technologies and strategies in the commercial and institutional building design and construction market through NEEA's BetterBricks program. Each lab is charged with developing regionally appropriate research, professional technical assistance, and design support, while at the same time supporting applied research and teaching climate-responsive and integrated design principles to current and the next generation of designers. This type of direct design-assistance program appears to be unique in the United States. One of the core activities of each lab is to offer technical support in daylighting design and integration with electric lighting.

The following text provides the context for the daylighting design collaborations that contributed to the projects included in this book. It explains the processes by which the Lab Network collaborates with the design profession and is offered in the hope that similar daylighting design collaborations could also occur in regions other than the Pacific Northwest.

meet at least 50 percent of the ambient lighting needs across annual daylight hours or the expected occupied periods. Second, designers develop tolerance levels for direct sunlight, contrast, and glare based on the need for visual acuity within each space or workstation area. The team establishes criteria for acceptable locations and duration of direct sunlight penetration into interior spaces based on occupancy times, thermal performance goals, and visual comfort requirements.

The term "illuminance" refers to the intensity of luminous flux incident upon a surface per unit area at any given point and is usually expressed as foot-candles (fc) or lux. However, human perception of space is better understood in terms of luminance. The term "luminance" (candelas per meter squared, or cd/m^2) refers to the luminous intensity of a surface in a given direction per unit of projected area and describes the brightness of light sources and illuminated surfaces. Luminance can be used to express the range of contrast experienced in a particular scene from a specific point of view. Luminance results from a light source itself or the interplay of a light source with the surface it strikes. The design of effective luminous distribution merges the art of spatial and material composition with the science of visual comfort. Effective daylighting must meet illuminance criteria while also maintaining effective luminance distribution as the sky brightness changes and the sun's position moves over time. Since daylight is, at its core, a visual experience, it is best represented through visual means. Therefore, the labs have specialized in creating methodologies for quickly representing the range of visual experiences expected within a hypothetical building and developed extensive capabilities in numerical data collection, photography of physical space and models, and computer simulation.

TOOLS AND METHODS

The Lab Network provides a technical platform on which to test design concepts, refine rules of thumb for addressing a regional context, and build an improved daylighting design intuition. To do this, it provides a center for hands-on design research where students, design professionals, and academic faculty engage one another while using simulation tools for testing daylighting and making other energy-related design decisions. The tools are both physical and digital and span multiple disciplines, including lighting, daylighting, heating, cooling, ventilation, and energy simulation. The labs assist architects with the formulation of daylighting design concepts through collaborative consultation on building organization, aperture design, and section geometry. Testing design options is central to this process, and the labs use a variety of methods to collect building performance data relative to the physical phenomena associated with daylight, sunlight, and human perception.

PHYSICAL DAYLIGHTING MODELS

The labs have historically specialized in the use of physical models to test architectural design concepts. Physical daylight models are simple to construct and can provide immediate real-time feedback. The labs have developed specifications for the construction of models that deliver accurate and meaningful simulation results.[1] These include recommendations for surface reflectance characteristics of interior model materials, appropriate levels of detail and scale, and techniques for instrumentation and data collection that do not interfere with simulation outcomes.

Designers use a physical model on a heliodon sun simulator in order to identify the location, duration, and geometric patterns of direct sunlight. Understanding these patterns facilitates improved design that avoids glare from the disc of the sun, manages heat gain, and directs the refinement of external solar-shading devices. Typically, the labs use a heliodon to investigate sun patterns over time on key dates (solstices and equinoxes). They capture the extent of sunlight across a day, in time-lapse format, with a digital video camera inserted into the model, as the heliodon moves though

Physical model on a computer-controlled, motorized "tilting earth" heliodon. Photo: K. Van Den Wymelenberg.

Physical model tests using a heliodon under real-sky conditions. Photo: C. Meek.

Skylight materiality and light distribution tests (transparent) and glare studies using scale models under real-sky conditions. Model: NBBJ Architects. Photo: C. Meek.

Same model with translucent skylight glazing to provide diffusion and glare control. Model: NBBJ Architects. Photo: C. Meek.

the range of solar exposures given a specific latitude and day of the year. With this information, designers and building owners are able to visualize annual solar exposure.

The same physical models can be used to assess the performance of spaces under overcast skies in a mirror-box overcast-sky simulator. Using mirrors and electric lights, this test chamber generates a simulated dome of light that is three times brighter at the zenith than it is at the horizon. It approximates the distribution of a sky dome on an overcast day and can help designers understand the luminous relationship between the proposed building apertures and the interior surface of a space under these conditions. With this tool, it is possible to quickly answer questions such as: Is the daylight distribution appropriately uniform? Does it provide a pleasing composition of light and dark within the architectural volume? Does the distribution reflect the visual needs of building users and the specific tasks and activities that they are engaged in? Using physical models to assess

design alternatives provides real-time input to designers who can observe the scale models directly with their eyes. Physical models enable immediate feedback and facilitate collaboration by allowing for quick dissemination of performance data to those without any technical experience in lighting. Designers do not need to wait for renderings to be processed and can avoid the lighting distortions that occur when viewing results on even the best computer monitors. This supports rapid iteration and quick decision making. However, physical models are limited when analyzing complex materials, can assess only one moment of a day or month at a time, and only analyze glare simplistically.

The labs communicate performance data derived from a mirror-box sky (or a model tested under real-sky conditions) with an array of photocells for measuring illuminance data. Traditionally, the labs have captured qualitative data about the distribution of light within an interior volume in still photography, using a single-lens reflex camera that is calibrated to the test chamber

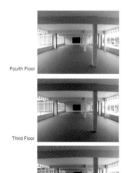

Fourth Floor

Third Floor

Second Floor

First Floor

Overcast Sky Simulation

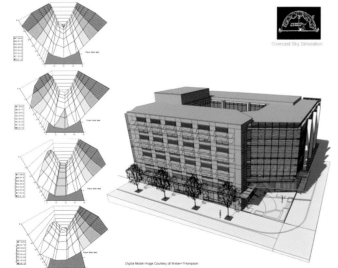

Digital Model Image Courtesy of Weber+Thompson

Physical model in mirror-box overcast sky.
Photo: H. Burpee.

Light distribution in a winery outbuilding under
overcast skies. Model: Boxwood Architects.
Photo: C. Meek.

Testing placement of artwork in a daylit environment using physical models. Model: Olson
Kundig Architects. Photo: C. Meek.

Physical and digital model simulations and
daylight factor data for the Terry Thomas Building. Model: Weber + Thompson Architects.
Photo: C. Meek.

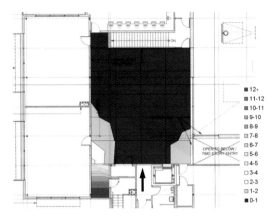

Multiple skylight configurations with resulting qualitative light distribution photographs and quantitative illuminance data at Rainier Vista Teen Center. Model: Weinstein AIU. Photo and diagram: University of Washington Integrated Design Lab.

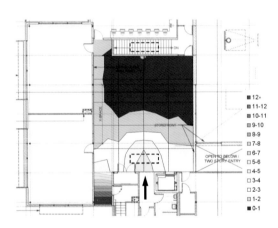

Translucent wall backlit with overhead skylight. Model: Weinstein AIU. Photo and diagram: University of Washington Integrated Design Lab.

and the model. More recently, they use high dynamic range (HDR) photography, which can produce images that better represent human visual experience. It is possible to use HDR photography to provide per-pixel luminance data, but with physical models, it is not common to use the actual materials (such as glazing products). However, even relatively simple physical models provide luminance data for making basic empirical comparisons of the luminous distribution of daylight within a series of design options.

DIGITAL DAYLIGHTING MODELS

Digital simulation models can answer different types of questions, including, How does the design perform under annual weather conditions, and what are the glare concerns and how severe are they? Digital tools can also support the types of questions listed above such as, Is the daylight distribution appropriately uniform? However, the qualitative data are always

Translucent wall frontlit with overhead skylight. Model: Weinstein AIU. Photo and diagram: University of Washington Integrated Design Lab.

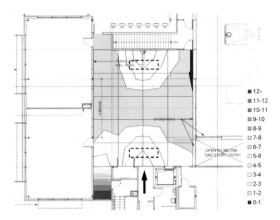

Center of space illuminated with rectangular diffuse overhead skylight. Model: Weinstein AIU. Photo and diagram: University of Washington Integrated Design Lab.

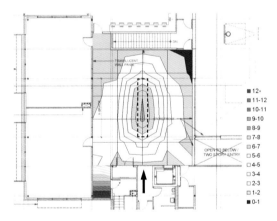

presented through the lens of the computer monitor, which can make them misleading. The development of digital tools for daylight simulation opens up the opportunity to collect substantially more information about a particular design or site location and interrelationships with other building systems. Advanced material specifications that would be nearly impossible to re-create with physical models are readily possible with digital models, and more complex material definitions are quickly becoming more available.

Simulation tools can help designers quickly understand solar exposure and direct sunlight penetration for the most complex geometries.[2] Widely accessible tools provide broad access to collections of regional weather data that can assist in design decision making.[3] New metrics and digital sky models allow for annualized assessment of daylight performance based on sky conditions recorded in long-term weather data.[4]

Regardless of the simulation technique, any model testing process must reflect the specific design questions being posed, and the resulting data must be effective in supporting design decision making. The labs continually work with designers to develop specific methodologies for conducting these technical analyses in a manner that meets design process objectives within project and timeline constraints. The following types of data can help answer most common daylighting design questions.

Shadow-casting studies using digital models to develop and test horizontal shading devices. Model: ZGF Architects. Rendering: C. Meek.

Simple Shadow Casting

Solar exposure can be expressed as a simple binary metric over time. Either direct sunlight is present or it is not. Site scale shadow studies can quickly identify the periods of site overshadowing caused by adjacent buildings and vegetation. Simple shadow-casting tools can determine the location, shape, and duration of patterns of direct sunlight within an interior space and are available with most three-dimensional modeling software packages or with a heliodon sun simulator. The presence of direct sun, or line of sight to the disc of the sun, serves as a simplified proxy for glare potential since for most visual tasks, the immediate presence of direct-beam sunlight correlates with visual discomfort. Additionally, the presence of direct sunlight during periods when a building is likely to be in cooling mode (e.g., warm summer afternoons) may also suggest the need for additional shading in order to avoid unwanted solar heat gain.

Instantaneous Measurements Data (Illuminance and Luminance)

The luminous distribution of daylight and sunlight within an interior at any given point in time can be described in terms of both illuminance and luminance. These data give the design team an instantaneous assessment of how much light is present at any given location, what the distribution of light is like across an interior volume, and what the composition of light will be on key architectural surfaces at a single point in time. Typically, the labs collect these data on key design days (equinoxes, solstices, or other dates specific to a building's expected occupancy) under both clear and overcast

Shadow-casting studies using digital models to develop automated blinds schedule. Model: ZGF Architects. Rendering: C. Meek.

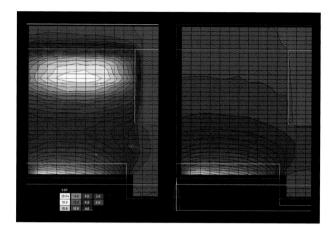

Overcast sky, 21 December at noon

Horizontal illuminance data comparison from digital models using Radiance software. Model: TCF Architecture. Illuminance image: Florian Piton/University of Washington Integrated Design Lab.

Luminance renderings and false color data comparison from digital models using Radiance. Model: TCF Architecture. False color image: Florian Piton/University of Washington Integrated Design Lab.

False color glare analysis using digital model and Radiance software. Model: ZGF Architects/University of Washington Integrated Design Lab. False color image: C. Meek.

skies. For projects located where skies are expected to be overcast for the majority of the occupied time, daylight factors (DF), or the percentage of outdoor illumination available indoors under a standardized overcast sky, are calculated and can be quickly converted into expected illuminance ranges across the year using typical annual outdoor illumination ranges for a given site location. Developing a complete picture of the luminous experience of the space as it changes across the day and year is of critical importance.

Annual Performance Data
Relatively new computer simulation techniques enable designers to calculate illuminance values on an annual basis relative to daylight performance goals using a digital model, weather data, and standardized sky models.[5] One annualized daylighting metric is daylight autonomy (DA), which is expressed as the percentage of a point's occupied time that daylight illuminance levels exceed a minimum criterion. For example, a point in a classroom with a DA of 50 percent would have sufficient daylight to meet minimum illumination goals (thirty-five foot-candles, for example) for half of the occupied hours on an annual basis. If this condition was met across a whole space, it would indicate the potential to achieve roughly 50 percent

lighting power savings with appropriate lighting controls in that space. This type of simulation is possible only with digital simulation tools and should be combined with other measures, such as direct sunlight patterns and point-in-time renderings, so as to ensure visual comfort.

Incident Solar Radiation

Using digital simulation tools to calculate incident solar radiation can help designers evaluate the effectiveness of exterior shading devices in reducing solar gain at a given surface (usually measured in btu/sf or W/m^2). The combination of reductions in incident solar radiation and rejection of direct sunlight can be used to characterize the capacity of shading devices to prevent glare and overheating. It should be noted, however, that these are two distinct phenomena and must be assessed individually as well as together. This is because solar shading seeks to control direct sunlight in order to avoid increased cooling loads, while glare control seeks to eliminate excessive contrast (often caused by direct sunlight) whenever occupants are present.

Technical Reports and Comparative Analysis

With the exponential increase in potential simulation output data, the ability to synthesize relevant data into a coherent summary suitable for formulating design decisions becomes a critical skill. The labs seek to find ways of creating the necessary data more rapidly, evaluating, and, most important, communicating these data in a way that is understandable and compelling to those whose expertise lies elsewhere. Sometimes, simply showing the visual difference between a space that is designed with effective daylight apertures and the same space without these elements gives a clear and immediate understanding to an owner who may not otherwise understand the importance of the proposed strategies.

At other times, design decisions (such as selecting materials or providing glare mitigation) must be supported with output having accurate absolute values. The role of the Lab Network is to provide guidance regarding the type of data that is most useful and to help the design team interpret these data in order to support design decisions. The labs document and communicate simulation results in technical reports that evaluate design decisions for energy and visual comfort performance and often recommend further testing and alternate design cases.

Sample Library

In their efforts to offer the most up-to-date technical assistance to design teams, the labs maintain samples of glazing technology, blinds, shades, and skylights as well as electric lighting and control systems. These are offered as stand-alone samples and are also integrated into the labs as demonstrations of the technologies. Keeping these libraries and displays current requires routine attention and funding.

Post-occupancy Assessment and Tool Lending

Learning from constructed projects through measurement, verification, and post-occupancy assessment is critical to developing new knowledge and refining design objectives. The labs strive to do post-occupancy assessment on all of the projects in which they are involved. This frequently takes the form of partnerships with design teams, so that they can evaluate the performance of a given project and identify lessons learned, and includes measuring luminance and illuminance ranges, occupant satisfaction, and energy performance. Each lab maintains a tool library of cameras and luminance and illuminance meters and, in some cases, a range of other equipment such as energy, airflow, temperature and relative humidity meters, and data loggers. These tools are deployed for post-occupancy assessments and other research projects and are also made available to architects, engineers, building operators, and others for help in diagnosing or troubleshooting building comfort and energy-related issues.

Gymnasium model with slot clerestory window. Model: Weinstein AIU. Photo: Max Foley/University of Washington Integrated Design Lab.

Rendering of desk layout in typical sidelit office building using Radiance. Rendering: University of Washington Integrated Design Lab. and University of Idaho Integrated Design Lab.

Gymnasium model with skylights and translucent baffles. Model: Weinstein AIU. Photo: Max Foley/University of Washington Integrated Design Lab.

False color luminance map of desk layout in typical sidelit office building. False color image: University of Washington Integrated Design Lab and University of Idaho Integrated Design Lab.

Gymnasium model with translucent skylights. Model: Weinstein AIU. Photo: Max Foley/University of Washington Integrated Design Lab.

Radiance rendering of seventy-two-inch-high partitions in typical sidelit office building. Rendering: University of Washington Integrated Design Lab and University of Idaho Integrated Design Lab.

False color luminance map of seventy-two-inch-high partitions in typical sidelit office building. Image: University of Washington Integrated Design Lab and University of Idaho Integrated Design Lab.

Testing darkening shade configurations with physical models. Model: Miller Hull Partnership. Photo: Max Foley/University of Washington Integrated Design Lab.

ESTABLISHING A LAB

There are documents available that offer useful guidance to those interested in developing capabilities similar to those of the Lab Network.[6] Most colleges of architecture or engineering at major universities have faculty with the expertise needed to develop a similar effort, given adequate funding. Most of the funding the Lab Network receives to perform the activities described in this text is provided either directly or indirectly by electric utilities and, to some extent, natural gas utilities. Utility funding usually comes with the requirement to document the energy savings that these programs can claim. This requires careful record keeping and long-term relationships with the building projects and design teams in order to secure these data. A prudent investigator will have detailed conversations with utilities about their expectations in terms of energy savings and will need to make clear that the timelines for achieving these 'market transformation' savings will be longer than those associated with standard energy-efficiency incentive programs.

While budgets and faculty time commitments of the individual universities within the Lab Network vary widely, dedicating 50 percent of a faculty's position description to this activity and securing funding for one or two graduate students represent a minimum commitment for starting this type of lab. With recent developments in digital simulation tools and software interfaces, very little up-front investment is needed. The daylighting calculation engine Radiance is freely available,[7] and users who have not had direct experience with it can use multiple low-cost and no-cost interfaces to access it. The cost of building an overcast-sky simulator and heliodon can vary widely, as they are usually built from shop drawings, due to the limited number and occasional lack of commercial manufacturers for these unique tools.

Post-occupancy assessment of daylight performance at the Terry Thomas Building using luminance maps from high dynamic range images taken for this book project. Photo: C. Meek and K. Van Den Wymelenberg.

High dynamic range photograph of Integrated Design Associates (IDeAs) office building in San Jose, California, used in developing the Daylighting Pattern Guide. Photo: University of Washington Integrated Design Lab and University of Idaho Integrated Design Lab.

High dynamic range computer simulation image of Integrated Design Associates (IDeAs) office building generated from a digital Radiance model. Photo: University of Washington Integrated Design Lab and University of Idaho Integrated Design Lab.

CONCLUSION

The Lab Network provides an applied research setting that helps address a split between designers and scientists that is often found in colleges of architecture and in the profession as a whole. As Professor G. Z. Brown observes in his essay "Delight in Sun, Wind, and Light," "At the root of the problem is the way architects think about and design buildings. Most people have a predilection for either humanistic or scientific thinking, and our educational systems reinforce this split. Design courses are dominated by humanistic thinking, while performance issues are covered in science-based technical courses. This results in an emphasis on *either* the humanistic *or* the performative aspects of buildings—not both—a way of thinking then carried into practice."[8] Lab Network staff work to bridge the gap between architectural designers and building scientists by providing technical input that helps shape the design process, whether in professional or academic settings. Presenting daylighting analysis data both qualitatively, via renderings and photographs, and quantitatively, via illuminance and luminance maps, is an effective way of breaking down walls between design and science. These technical scientific analyses provide a rich and meaningful source of knowledge that can be used to guide the creative design process while broadening the scope of inquiry to include climate and patterns of light when formulating architectural solutions.

Universities are well positioned to serve as conduits for collaboration and innovation. The synergies driven, in part, by the Lab Network have led to profound collaborations among distinct disciplines, resulting in technological and strategic innovations in both product and process. It has helped build a well-traveled bridge between practice and academia. And perhaps most important, it has helped lead to the creation of memorable experiences of architecture, as described by Juhani Pallasmaa:

In memorable experiences of architecture, space, matter and time fuse into one single dimension, into the basic structure of being, that penetrates the consciousness. We identify ourselves with this space, this place, this moment and these dimensions as they become ingredients of our very existence.[9]

Notes

INTRODUCTION

1 Henry David Thoreau, *Atlantic Monthly* 9, no. 56 (June 1862).

2 David E. Miller, *Toward a New Regionalism: Environmental Architecture in the Pacific Northwest* (Seattle: University of Washington Press, 2005).

3 Cliff Mass, *The Weather of the Pacific Northwest* (Seattle: University of Washington Press, 2008), 3.

4 4. Ibid., 9–10.

5 David. W. Orr, *Design on the Edge: The Making of a High-Performance Building* (Cambridge, MA: The MIT Press, 2008).

6 On education and work environments, see Heschong Mahone Group, *Windows and Classrooms: A Study of Student Performance and the Indoor Environment* (Fair Oaks, CA: Heschong Mahone Group, 2003). On healing, see J. M. Walch et al., "The Effect of Sunlight on Postoperative Analgesic Medication Use: A Prospective Study of Patients Undergoing Spinal Surgery," *Psychosomatic Medicine* (January 1, 2005).

7 Todd S. Horowitz et al., "Efficacy of Bright Light and Sleep/Darkness Scheduling in Alleviating Circadian Maladaptation to Night Work," *American Journal of Physiology, Endocrinology, and Metabolism* 281, no. 2 (2001): E384–91.

8 Karin Knorr Cetina, "The Couch, the Cathedral, and the Laboratory: On the Relationship between Experiment and Laboratory in Science," in *Science as Practice and Culture* (Chicago: University of Chicago Press, 1992), 113–38.

PROJECTS

1 "Jim Olson, FAIA," Olson Kundig Architects, at Architonic, http://www.architonic.com/aiabt/olson-kundig-architects/5204770.

2 Novelty Hill Wines, accessed January 31, 2011, http://www.noveltyhillwines.com.

3 HistoryLink.org, accessed January 31, 2011, http://www.historylink.org/index.cfm?DisplayPage=output.cfm&file_id=4169.

DESIGNING WITH THE LIGHT OF PLACE

1   G. Z. Brown and Jeff Cole, *Rethinking the Design Process* (Portland: Energy Studies in Buildings Laboratory, University of Oregon, and Konstrukt, 2006) completed for Better-Bricks/NEEA (available from www.betterbricks.com).

2   Michael Benedikt, "Environmental Stoicism and Place Machismo," *Harvard Design Magazine* (Winter–Spring 2002).

APPENDIX

1   Christopher Meek and Kevin G. Van Den Wymelenberg, "Building Daylighting Models," Integrated Design Lab Puget Sound, University of Washington, 2004, http://www.integrateddesignlab.com/Seattle/Resources/Documents/Building_Daylighting_Models.pdf.

2   Google SketchUp, accessed January 31, 2011, http://sketchup.google.com/download/#utm_campaign=en&utm_source=en-ha-na-us-google&utm_medium=ha&utm_term=SketchUp . See also Autodesk, "Autodesk Ecotect Analysis," accessed January 31, 2011, http://usa.autodesk.com/adsk/servlet/pc/index?id=12602821&siteID=123112.

3   "EnergyPlus Energy Simulation Software: Weather Data," accessed January 16, 2011, http://apps1.eere.energy.gov/buildings/energyplus/cfm/weather_data.cfm. See also Murray Milne, "Energy Design Tools," accessed March 13, 2009, http://www2.aud.ucla.edu/energy-design-tools.

4   Christoph F. Reinhart, John Mardaljevic, and Zack Rogers, "Dynamic Daylight Performance Metrics for Sustainable Building Design," *Leukos* 3, no. 1 (July 2006): 7–31.

5   John Mardaljevic, "Daylight Simulation: Validation, Sky Models and Daylight Coefficients," De Montfort University, Leicester, UK, December 1999.

6   See Kevin G. Van Den Wymelenberg, Joel Loveland, and Christopher Meek, *Daylighting Lab Operation and Management Plan*, Rensselaer Polytechnic Institute, Lighting Research Center, Troy, NY, 2005, www.lrc.rpi.edu/programs/daylighting/pdf/labopmngmntplan.pdf; and Kevin G. Van Den Wymelenberg, Jim Coles, Ery Djunaedy, and Brad Acker, "Design Lab: Exploring Synergies of Outreach, Research and Teaching While Innovating Classroom Design," in *ACSA 2009 Annual Meeting Proceedings*.

7   G. Ward, The RADIANCE 3.5 Synthetic Imaging System, 2003, accessed May 27, 2009, http://radsite.lbl.gov/radiance/refer/ray.html.

8   G. Z. Brown, "Delight in Sun, Wind, and Light: Sustainability and Pleasure Indoors/Outdoors," *Harvard Design Magazine* (Spring–Summer 2009).

9   Juhani Pallasmaa, *The Eyes of the Skin: Architecture and the Senses*, 2d ed. (Seattle: Academy Press, 2005).

Index

Page numbers in italic type refer to illustrations.